D1520918

EFTS

MARK G. BENDER

EFTS

ELECTRONIC FUNDS TRANSFER SYSTEMS

ELEMENTS and IMPACT

KENNIKAT PRESS ● 1975
Port Washington, New York ● London

The publisher and the National Consumer Finance Association acknowledge with gratitude the cooperation of the following persons and agencies in allowing use of their materials:

Arthur D. Little, Inc.: Tables 2-1 and 3-2; American Bankers Association: Figure 2-3 which appeared in *Banking,* May 1974, Table 2-2 which appeared in *Banking,* December 1974; and Practicing Law Institute and Mr. L. Richard Fischer: Figures 3-1, 3-2, and 3-3.

Manufactured in the United States of America

Published by
Kennikat Press Corp.
Port Washington, N.Y./London

TO MY PARENTS

CONTENTS

TABLES AND FIGURES

PREFACE

Over the past several years there has been a significant increase in the application of advanced computer and communication technologies to the age-old problem of effecting economic exchange. Spurred on by the experiments and programs of both the private and public sectors our society is rapidly advancing toward that day when electronic impulses will largely replace coins, currency, and checks as our major media of exchange. Furthermore, the advent of electronic funds transfer systems appears to portend revolutionary changes in traditional economic and social relationships—changes which will far transcend those historically associated with the evolution of the exchange mechanism.

Yet in spite of the growing amount of awareness and interest in EFTS, little has been done to provide the non-expert with a relatively comprehensive analysis of the many facets of the electronic payments phenomenon. This study is designed to fill in that informational gap and to do so in a non-technical, readable manner.

More specifically, this survey will discuss the major forces which have precipitated the transition to an electronic payments mechanism; the major elements of that mechanism; some of the attendant issues involved; and the probable economic implications. This book will have served its purpose, then, if the reader gains reasonable insight into the overall development, structure, and impact of the progressing changeover to EFTS.

It is with great pleasure that I acknowledge the comments and the encouragement of my colleagues Carl F. Hawver, S. Lees Booth, Robert B. Norris, and Vernon Evans from the inception through to maturation of this project. Robert L. Harlow, my good friend and colleague, was also generous enough to read and comment on the entire manuscript. Certainly, this undertaking could never have been completed quite as rapidly or as smoothly without the excellent secretarial assistance of Sharon Gover. Karolin Blackson proved to be an invaluable editor while Romena Johnson helped with typing and editing whenever the timetable was threatened. Others, too numerous to mention, also contributed time and effort to assure the success of this book.

But my greatest debt is to my wife Ana Maria who in so many ways made it all worthwhile.

EFTS

CHAPTER 1

EXCHANGE MECHANISMS
IN RETROSPECT

A careful investigation of economic history would indicate that the evolution of exchange mechanisms has been inseparable from the evolution of economic society itself. Indeed, advances in economic society have consistently precipitated advances in the exchange mechanism of that society so that the latter would facilitate rather than restrain economic activity.

It is not surprising that as economic society progressed from the primitive-agrarian state, to the commercial-industrial state, and now to the post-industrial state that the exchange mechanism required to accommodate such a society has itself progressed. And just as the dynamics of economic evolution have continually altered the relative importance of specific sectors, interest groups, and individuals in society, so too, have such relationships been altered among all of those financial institutions subjected to the concomitant dynamics of the exchange mechanism.

Barter Exchange

Few are the readers who have not been exposed at one time or another to the essential characteristics of primitive societies and their unique system of exchange known as simple or direct barter.

In order to have the advantages of some specialized production as well as the fulfillment of the diverse needs and wants of their populace, primitive societies made use of an exchange mechanism in which goods were exchanged directly for goods. In this way individuals, as both producers and consumers, could bring to market that commodity which they had in excess and exchange it directly for that commodity in which they were deficient.

The simple barter system, however, was characterized by numerous inefficiencies. For example, above all else a barter system requires a bilateral or dual coincidence of wants before either party to a transaction can benefit from exchange.[1] In addition, the time-effort expended in searching for a trading partner could be very costly if not altogether prohibitive on occasion, while the extent of the market, and thereby the extent of trade possibilities, was severely limited by the portability of the barter commodity. Finally, the simple barter system could not easily provide for a systematic method of deferred payment, simply because of the lack of durability of a wide range of bartered commodities.

Modified Barter Exchange

The growth of the primitive-agrarian society in terms of population, production, communication, and trading areas, exerted irresistible pressures on the simple barter system with its obvious fetters on production and consumption possibilities. In time, therefore, the exchange mechanism itself evolved so as to accommodate the new demands of economic society.

The second stage of barter exchange is often referred to as modified or indirect barter. The essential characteristic of this exchange mechanism was the substitution of a single exchange commodity for the array of commodities used in the simple barter system. In essence, the advancing society collectively decided upon a specific commodity to serve as a medium of exchange.

In most cases the specialized commodity medium of exchange of the indirect barter system had a number of advantages over the various commodities of simple barter: the commodity medium was widely desirable or acceptable for both its use value and its exchange value so as to result in significant time-effort or search-cost savings; it was sufficiently portable to substantially reduce the transportation or transfer costs of payment; it was divisible enough to effect exchanges of small as well as large values; finally, it was durable and allowed for deferred payments.

The gains to economic society which were derived from the first major advance in the exchange mechanism were for the most part centered in the savings of the time and the expense heretofore necessitated by simple barter, as well as in the substitution of multilateral exchange for the bilateral exchange limitations of the earlier mechanism. In short, the advent of modified barter allowed a progressing society to economize in the use of its resources for production as well as to increase the community's welfare through a greater number of more complex consumption alternatives.

Money Based Exchange

The specialized commodity medium of exchange frequently had a use value in direct consumption but more often than not the use value was related to the decorative characteristics of the exchange medium. Such was the case with the precious metals, especially gold and silver, which gained widespread acceptance as exchange media in the very early stages of economic development.

The precious metals were not only characterized by acceptability, durability, portability, and divisibility but they went beyond that and gradually assumed all of the essential roles of money. That is, the precious metals constituted: (1) a medium of exchange by which transfers of economic goods or services could be efficiently effected; (2) a unit of account in terms of which the relative values of different goods and services could be stated; (3) a store of value through which means saving or accumulation of purchasing power was facilitated; and finally, (4) a means of deferred payment which allowed for the optimization of current production and consumption without the constraint of necessity of immediate payment.

The monetary role of the precious metals was greatly strengthened by the tendency of the emerging central governments of expanding political entities to undertake the minting or coinage of those metals on an official and systematic basis. Coinage represented governments' assumption of the power and the responsibility to shape economic society by supplying and managing the new lifeblood of that society—its monetary medium of exchange.

Elementary Banking

Each successive advance of economic society has altered the balance of economic power within that society. And as economies became progressively more commercial in nature, the balance of economic power shifted accordingly. Significantly expanded trading areas, a remarkably growing volume and value of exchange, and the accumulation of monetary wealth, characterized the new economics. And the emergence of an influential mercantile class shaped the new politics.

To accommodate the needs of the mercantilists, who devoted their energies to the promotion of exchange and the accumulation of capital, a system of money warehouses gradually evolved. These warehouses were located in the major trading centers of most nation-states and initially served as depositories for the safe-keeping of the funds of the commercial class. The warehouse would simply issue a receipt to those who opened a deposit account and upon presentation of such a receipt the warehouse would return the specified sum to the depositor.

It was not long, however, before traders found that the warehouse receipts in and of themselves could be a convenient means of payment. As long as the warehouse receipt was 100 percent backed by "gold," for example, then it was considered as good as gold by the holder and certainly more convenient. To effect payment a receipt needed only to be signed over from one deposit account holder to another. Upon presentation of the receipt the warehouse would transfer the specified sum of funds between accounts as directed.

In return for their depository and transfer services the warehouses earned fees which were used to cover their costs as well as to provide their owners a profit. In short, the warehouses constituted an elementary banking system, characteristics of which are still with us today.

Fractional Reserves

The ever-quickening pace of commerce in conjunction with the new forces of manufacture and industrialization severely strained the capacity of an exchange system based on a government-controlled commodity money supply and the most simple of financial intermediaries. The development of fractional reserve banking and the government issue of fiat money constituted the adaptation of the exchange mechanism to the economic realities.

Since it was unlikely that all holders of warehouse deposits would ever withdraw their funds at the same time, the warehouses began to issue their own drafts or bills-of-exchange which were themselves backed by the deposits of warehouse customers and also came to serve as media of exchange. The net result was a fractional reserve banking system: the funds on deposit at the banks (eventually to consist of nothing but government-issued "legal tender") were used to back up both the claims of depositors as well as the new debt obligations of those very same banks.

The growth of fractional reserve banking had a revolutionary impact on economic society. Money could now be "created" as the banking system extended credit through its own drafts, upon the demand of both producers and consumers, and at times upon the demand of government. Furthermore, the banking system developed a clearing house capacity which allowed the drafts issued by a bank in one trading center to be presented for payment at a bank in a geographically distant trading center. The latter bank would accept the draft, make payment, and then "clear" that draft back to the originating institution for reimbursement.

As a result of these payments-system developments, many of the heretofore extant constraints on production, consumption, trade, and investment were severed and the overall pace of economic growth accelerated accordingly.

Modern Exchange

The restructuring of the exchange mechanism along the modern lines now associated with industrial society was largely based on an expansion of the acceptability of that which constituted money. In fact, it is generally conceded that the simplicity or complexity of a given economic society is reflected in those things which are used as money by that society.

More specifically, money can be defined as anything which is commonly accepted in exchange for goods and services or, put differently, anything which can effect an exchange of value. Various societies have used different types of money and these monies at one time or another were commodities, precious metals, and more recently, a wide range of the debt obligations or promises-to-pay issued by both public and private institutions. In our own advanced economy the monetary obligations of government, known as legal tender, consist of coins and paper currency while the debt obligations of banks are commonly known as demand deposits or checking account deposits.

The sum total of coins, currency and demand deposits held by the non-bank public formally constitutes our money supply with demand deposits representing by far the single most important component of that money supply. Practically speaking, however, there are additional means by which exchanges of value can be effected. For example, credit cards, travelers' checks, and other financial instruments are so easily used for exchange purposes that most individuals will often treat them as simply another component of their money supply.

But in spite of the complexity of our current exchange mechanism the signposts of change are again on the horizon and all of them are pointing to EFTS.

CHAPTER 2

FORCES OF TRANSITION

The coin, currency, and demand deposit payments mechanism familiar to most readers has flourished for a number of decades. The use of demand deposits, or checks, accelerated in the post World War II years because of their convenience, safety, and efficiency in effecting payments transfers, not to mention their widespread acceptance by the public. But in recent years the rising costs of handling paper transfers, the availability of the required technology, and the combined pressures for change from both public and private institutions have all come together to both precipitate and facilitate another major change in the payments mechanism: electronic funds transfers.

Current Payments System Costs

The current payments mechanism is one based on effecting an exchange of value by means of coin, paper currency, checks, and to a much lesser extent by credit cards, letters of credit, travelers' checks, bank drafts, and so on. Arthur D. Little, Inc., in a report prepared for the National Science Foundation, has estimated the overall cost of this payments system in the mid 1970s to be in the neighborhood of at least $14.2 billion.[1] The major portion of this cost, some $11 billion, was accounted for by the coin, currency, and check components of the money supply.

Coin and Currency. The utilization of coin and currency as a means of effecting payments has some rather obvious cost elements. For example, the coins and the paper currency incur the direct costs of production. In addition, they require expenditures for recording, packaging, distribution, cleaning, and ultimately, destruction. Other, more indirect costs of using a coin and currency payments system, involve the expenditures on the safe-keeping or protection of such monies, insurance, and finally expenditures related to the problems of counterfeiting, robbery, and other crimes. Table 2-1 shows that the cost of supporting this cash component of the payments system has been estimated to be about $3 billion. However, the approximate 6 percent per year growth in paper money alone suggests that this cost will increase substantially during the remainder of the 1970s.

Checks. The demand deposit, or check-based component of the payments system has assumed the major burden of effecting exchanges of value. It has been estimated that approximately 22.5 billion checks were written on demand deposit accounts in the United States in 1970 and, furthermore, that the growth of check volume is in the neighborhood of 7 percent per year, projecting check volume in 1980 of about 45 billion.[2]

The total cost of operating the check-based system is high and is related to such elements as the direct production of checks, the verification of checking account holders, the authorization of payments by check, the costs of transferring and handling checks and of providing their related account statements, and finally, the costs of float, forgery, fraud, time, and user inconvenience. All of these costs are borne in one form or other by all members of society and their total has been estimated to be $8 billion (see Table 2-1).

The problem of coping with a check-based payments system characterized by an increasing volume of transactions and steadily increasing cost has been of concern to the private and the public sectors of the economy. For example, as far back as 1968 the Hempstead Bank of Long Island, New York, designed a prototype remote terminal and electronic funds transfer system which has evolved into the currently

10

well-known Instant Transaction payments system.

Also in 1968 the American Bankers Association formed its Monetary and Payment Systems (MAPS) Planning Committee to study the problems and the opportunities which would be presented by the

Table 2-1

COSTS OF CURRENT PAYMENTS SYSTEM

(Annual Basis — Mid 1970s)

	Transactions (billions)	Cost per Transaction	Total Cost (billions)
CASH (COIN/CURRENCY)			
Direct Costs	—	—	0.45
Related Costs	—	—	2.50 c
Total			2.95 c
CHECKS			
Business/Government Preparation a	12	$ 0.15	1.80
Consumer Preparation a	12	0.10	1.20
Consumer Deposit a	4	0.10	0.40
Bank Processing	24	0.18	4.32
Other b	24	0.02	0.77
Total			8.20
CREDIT CARDS			
Sales Slip Processing and Billing	5.02	.55	2.76
Total			14.20

a. Includes mailing costs where applicable
b. Other covers elements such as FRB Clearing, etc.
c. Estimated allocation of shared costs
   Source: Arthur D. Little, Inc.

that a nationwide system for the electronic clearing and distribution of payments should be developed.[3] Furthermore, the Committee specifically recommended that the bank charge card should be comprehensively developed for electronic payments purposes; that a privately operated and competitive wire system must be maintained parallel to the Federal Reserve Wire; that commercial banks should closely monitor the payments needs of their customers; and that a set of standards should be developed for EFTS purposes.[4] In essence, the banking community was both endorsing and planning for electronic funds transfer.

The concern of the public sector about the cost and inconvenience of the check-based payments system was amply demonstrated in the following remarks by Senator Edward W. Brooke at the Payments System Policy Conference of the American Bankers Association in December, 1974:

. . . . it is clear that our commercial bank check payments mechanisms do need modernization. The Federal Reserve Board estimates that check volume is increasing at a rate that will double during the next decade from the current estimated level of 26 million items yearly. The total annual cost of clearing paper checks and using cash in our economy has been approximated at $10 billion, or about 1 percent of our gross national product. At present, the average paper check is cleared through a multistage process involving a substantial amount of manual labor. Processing costs have been estimated to be at least 16 cents per check. Unless there is a large scale transition to electronic funds transfers, the growth in check usage may eventually impede the flow of funds in the economy and make the use of checks slow and expensive for customers and banks alike.

The high cost of check-based exchange has been well established and must be considered as the single most important force exerting pressure for a revolutionary change in the payments system. In short, the alternatives are either to save many billions of dollars by automating the exchange of value or to suffer the losses associated with a relatively cumbersome exchange mechanism at the very foundation of our highly complex society.

Significant Innovations

Although the concept of an automated payments mechanism has only recently gained widespread attention, that should not be allowed to obscure the fact that a number of significant innovations have been introduced in the check-oriented system in past years. Indeed, such payments facilitating technologies as the Federal Reserve Wire, the Bank Wire, Regional Check Processing Centers, and the European-style GIRO (Greek work meaning "circle" or "ring") systems have provided the basic infrastructure for effecting a change from our current payments system to the electronic funds transfer systems of the future.

Federal Reserve Wire System. Perhaps the first major innovation in the automation of payments was the Federal Reserve Wire System. This system allows participating banks to clear interbank payments via teletype communications through their respective Regional Reserve Banks. According to the "Coding Differences" manual published by the Bank Administration Institute,[5]

The system is a credit transfer system. A transfer message by Bank A is an instruction to its Federal Reserve Bank to debit Bank A's account. The Federal Reserve Bank then credits the due-to account of a distant Federal Reserve Bank, which in turn credits the account of the receiving bank.

The Federal Reserve Wire System, which is centered in Culpeper, Virginia, represents a limited access model of an electronic funds transfer system. The twelve Reserve Banks, their 24 branches, the Federal Reserve Board, and the U.S. Treasury can all communicate with one another through Culpeper via high-speed data-carrying telephone lines, while member banks communicate with Regional Banks by teletype terminals.[6] Direct computer-to-computer communication throughout the wire system is the next logical step and is already being implemented. The net result, of course, will be nearly instantaneous funds transfer capability throughout the United States.

In a recent publication on the purposes and functions of the Federal Reserve System, the Board of Governors stated:[7]

The Federal Reserve also makes available to member banks a computer-based communications system that can be used to transfer funds from one part of the country to another swiftly and efficiently. All such transfers are made through debits or credits to member bank reserve accounts held at the Reserve Banks. Funds transferred on this network are immediately available to the receiving member bank upon receipt of an advice. Member banks may also use the communications system to transfer funds to and from specific customer accounts by providing the necessary information in the transfer request. The System's communications facilities permit member banks to lend their excess reserves to banks that are experiencing temporary reserve deficiencies. The market that brings banks together in such transactions is called the Federal funds market.

The System's communications facilities may also be used to transfer marketable Government securities. Trading in these issues is very active, and transfer of ownership typically involves large-denomination certificates payable to bearer; in many instances such securities are held in the Reserve Banks for safekeeping. Serious problems may be encountered from time to time in the physical transfer of such securities between banks and dealers and between dealers and other investors and in the storage of these securities. To help resolve such problems, the Federal Reserve Banks and the Treasury have instituted a computerized book-entry system by which ownership of U. S. Treasury and certain Federal agency securities is recorded on the books of the Federal Reserve Banks, and transfers may be effected without the necessity of transporting the securities. Use of the Federal Reserve's communications system in combination with the book-entry system provides an efficient and secure method of transferring ownership of Government and agency securities and for making interest payments.

To summarize, the Federal Reserve System now has the capability to clear and settle accounts with member banks for both debits and credits whether by check or by wire or by the medium of magnetic tape. Furthermore, to accommodate different stages of payments development by different economic units, Reserve Offices will be capable of mixing payments media; that is, accepting payments in a form such as magnetic tape while making payments in paper form and vice versa.

According to Federal Reserve Board Governor George W. Mitchell, "The Federal Reserve's wire network—in addition to surface and air courier systems for the movement of paper—now provides the Federal Reserve with the capability to deliver payments by check, magnetic tape, hard copy, and wire form to any bank in the nation, and, for that matter to any other depository institution via a commercial bank."[8]

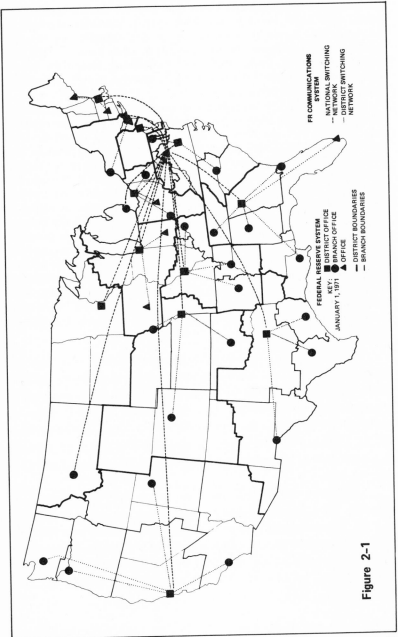

FR COMMUNICATIONS SYSTEM

NATIONAL SWITCHING NETWORK

DISTRICT SWITCHING NETWORK

FEDERAL RESERVE SYSTEM

KEY:
JANUARY 1, 1971

■ DISTRICT OFFICE
● BRANCH OFFICE
▲ OFFICE
— DISTRICT BOUNDARIES
— BRANCH BOUNDARIES

Figure 2-1

Bank Wire System. A system of funds transfer analogous to the above is the Bank Wire System which dates back to the early 1950s. This communications system was established by the private banking system initially to facilitate payments between a small number of Chicago and New York banks. Currently the Bank Wire System has expanded to include about 250 banks spread out across the country, all of which can relay both administrative and transfer messages to one another through "computer switching centers in New York and Chicago."[9]

Regional Check Processing. A more recent innovation in the check-based payments mechanism was initiated by the Federal Reserve in June, 1971, when it released a policy statement to the effect that the Federal Reserve System would undertake a two stage program to restructure the nation's payments mechanism with the help of electronic technology.

The first stage of the proposed restructuring had the objective of altering the check-clearing system in a way that would "result in faster, more convenient and more economical banking service to the public" through the establishment of a series of regional check processing centers (RCPCs). In combination with the recently developed magnetic ink character recognition code (MICR) which is imprinted directly on the check, the regional check processing centers allowed the Federal Reserve to require new time limits on check clearing by late 1972.[10] In effect, the MICR-coded checks permitted a more rapid transit of those checks to the RCPC concentration points for collection. As a result the speed and efficiency of check collection have greatly increased and the amount of float in the exchange system has decreased.

Again, according to the Board of Governors,[11]

The volume of checks handled by Federal Reserve Banks has grown rapidly in recent years. In 1973 the Reserve Banks cleared about 10 billion of the estimated 26 billion checks drawn on banks in the United States. Those checks not handled by the Federal Reserve are cleared by local clearinghouse associations, by large correspondent banks, or by direct local exchange. Settlement among banks for these check exchanges is often effected through the reserve accounts of member banks.

To reduce the time required to clear checks through the check collection system, the Federal Reserve has implemented a Regional Check Processing Centers program. This program has resulted in the establishment of Federal Reserve check-clearing offices in seven additional locations, and in a sharp increase in the number of checks cleared on an immediate-credit basis—from 19 percent prior to the program to 56 percent by the end of 1973.

The regional check processing center zones are concentrated in the East, West, and mid-West in basic alignment with the major population regions of the United States. More specifically, the Federal Reserve has overnight check clearing operations in 47 of the planned 50 major national trading areas. As a result, Federal Reserve check float has been decreased from the approximate $3 billion prior to the RCPC system to about $1.5 billion currently.[12] Actually, the Federal Reserve System is moving toward a clearing network which would virtually eliminate any float attributable to its own operations.

Finally, in November, 1973, the Federal Reserve set in motion the second stage of its restructuring program by inviting comments on the proposed changes in Regulation J regarding the use and operation of the Fed wire network and on the fundamental structure of the nation's payments mechanism. More specifically, the Fed solicited comments on the appropriate roles for itself and other institutions concerning the ownership, the control, and the costs of an electronic funds transfer system.

GIRO Transfer Systems. Unlike the situation in the United States, the postal services of some 44 countries have a direct involvement in third party payments. These GIRO systems, which transfer credits rather than (check) debits, basically use postal service offices, clearinghouses, and customer deposit accounts with the postal service to effect funds transfers.[13] The mechanics of the transfer are:

1. The payor brings in person or otherwise forwards a payment order to his local post office.
2. The local post office debits the payor's deposit account and forwards the transfer information to a postal system clearinghouse.
3. The clearinghouse debits the account of the payor's post office and credits the account of the payee's post office.
4. The payee's post office credits the account of, or otherwise forwards payment to, the payee.

EFTS

The flow of both funds and paper in existing GIRO systems is unidirectional—from payor to payee only—as will be the case in the future electronic funds transfer system. Furthermore, the GIRO system can exploit comprehensive geographic penetration as well as long established consumer confidence and familiarity with national postal services. It would not be surprising, therefore, to see the United States

Figure 2-2

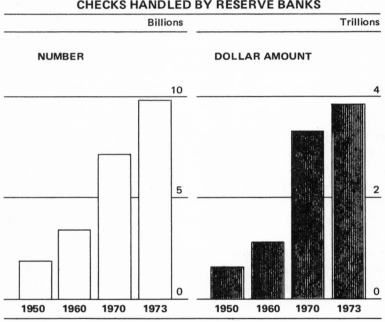

Figures exclude checks of the U.S. Govt. and postal money orders.
Source: Federal Reserve Board of Governors

Postal Service make vigorous efforts to establish a GIRO system, especially with the prospects of a drastic decrease in mail-based payments transfers in an EFTS environment.

All of the foregoing payments system innovations contributed greatly to the capability of current exchange mechanisms to meet the demands of economic society, but of even more importance

18

they have provided a base of technological familiarity and know-how which is now facilitating the transition to automated payments.

Thrift Institution Pressures

Additional and persistent pressures for change in the nation's payments mechanism have come in recent years from nonbank thrift institutions. The latter include savings and loan associations, mutual savings banks, and credit unions, all of which have shown increased interest in offering money transfer services out of savings accounts. Many of these thrift institutions have already amply demonstrated, in a number of significant experiments, their capacity to offer third party payment services in direct competition with the commercial banking system.

The NOW Account. The first major breakthrough to third party payments privileges for thrifts occurred in 1971 when the Wilmington Savings Fund Society of Delaware began to offer checking account services. These services were rapidly followed by a "complete financial services package" which included pre-authorized bill payment, that is, the "automatic transfer of funds out of a customer's checking account for the payment of specified mortgage loans, insurance premiums, and utility bills."[14]

But the most widely known thrift experiment with third party payments started in June, 1972, when the Consumers Savings Bank of Worcester, Massachusetts, introduced what are widely known as NOW accounts. By means of this negotiable order of withdrawal program the savings bank's customers had the privilege of writing "payable through" drafts against their interest-bearing savings accounts.[15]

The NOW account was the first systematic demonstration of the feasibility of and consumer interest in replacing both the demand deposit account and the savings account with a single dual function account. Technically speaking, the payment from the depositor's account is made by writing an order payable through the savings bank's account in a commercial bank which, after clearing, becomes a subsequent debit to the depositor's savings account. Practically speaking, the negotiable order of withdrawal is a check.[16]

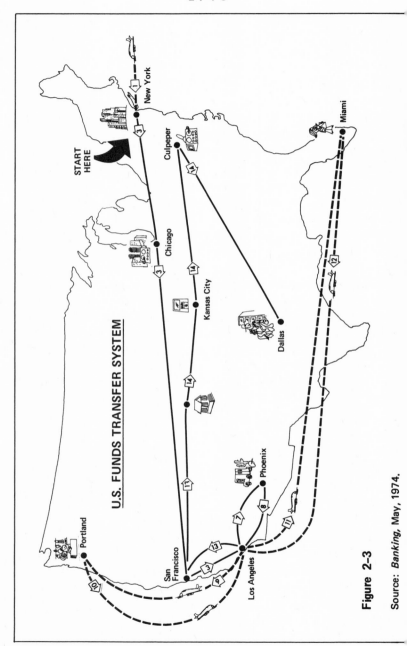

U.S. FUNDS TRANSFER SYSTEM

START HERE

New York

Culpeper

Chicago

Kansas City

Dallas

Miami

Phoenix

Portland

San Francisco

Los Angeles

Figure 2-3

Source: *Banking,* May, 1974.

1. Foreign bank says to New York Bank A: "Debit my account with you by $2 million and credit New York Bank B with $2 million." It airmailed instructions, but could have cabled.

• 2. In N.Y. Bank A accomplishes this transfer electronically through CHIPS, a system operated by NY Clearing House and servicing about 40 banking institutions, with 15 banks directly on line into the system. System was established primarily to handle international payments coming into the US. Volume can run as high as $40 billion a day. At end of day, movement of funds is summarized to show each bank's position in respect to each of the other banks in the system. The next morning, this information is given to the N.Y. Federal Reserve, which reflects these changes in balances in its own records.

3. At same time, foreign bank asks New York Bank B to forward $1 million to the XYZ Co. in Los Angeles, which it can do by Bank Wire message through switching at Chicago and San Francisco to its correspondent bank in L.A. Bank Wire is an organization of about 230 banks throughout the country and is managed by 9 NY and 5 Chicago banks. It is not a settlement system with a central clearing house, but works out funds transfers in terms of correspondent balances.

• 4. XYZ Co. may pay employees, as authorized by them, by a checkless system of CACHA (California Automated Clearing House Association). XYZ makes a tape of payment instructions and submits this to its bank, which strips off records of employees who have accounts with it—crediting their accounts—then forwards the tape to the ACH (automated clearing house), which distributes the remaining records to other employees' banks. Among them is John Dough. (More common procedure today is by traditional check.)

• 5. The following day, a quarterly payment is due on an insurance premium which Dough has pre-authorized. His insurance company has issued to the bank a draft saying in effect: "Debit his account, credit ours."

• 6. John Dough writes and mails a check to his grocery, which deposits the check with its bank, which happens to be the same as Dough's. Bank credits grocer's account, debits Dough's.

7. Dough writes and mails a check to a Phoenix motel, where he stayed last weekend. Motel deposits check in its bank.

*Not shown in map.

8. Phoenix bank, a member of the Federal Reserve System within the Los Angeles Regional Check Processing Area, dispatches check via courier service to Los Angeles RCPC, which credits Phoenix bank, debits Dough's Los Angeles bank and passes check on to it for its month-end accounting to Dough. (Alternatively, the Phoenix bank might send the check to a Los Angeles correspondent bank at a later hour for same-day credit.)

9. Dough writes to mail order outfitter in Portland, Ore., putting his bank card number on order form, as invited. Outfitter presents copy of order to his Portland bank for crediting to his account, with merchant's discount.

10. Portland bank mails order copy to a point specified by the bank issuing the card to Dough, later enters a cumulative draft covering this and various other items into the Fed clearing mechanism, against the card-issuing bank. That bank accumulates the charges against Dough's account and bills Dough monthly.

11. Dough mails check to daughter, who is a student at the University of Miami. She deposits check with her large Miami bank.

12. Miami bank notes that check is payable at a large Los Angeles bank it regularly does business with, puts check in envelope with several other checks and mails it to Dough's bank in Los Angeles. This is a direct-send correspondent credit-debit relationship for funds settlement, bypassing the Fed entirely. Miami bank could have sent check to Fed's Miami Regional Check Processing Center, which would have started it on its way to Dough's bank in LA.

13. Dough who is moving from Los Angeles to Denver, asks realtor selling his LA house to send the $50,000 proceeds—as soon as he receives them—by Fed wire to Dough's new account in Denver (so funds would be immediately available to him.)

14. Dough's new bank in Denver notes that this deposit to his account raises their reserve account with the Fed too high over the amount needed. It gets on the phone to find the best deal it can get for one day's use of $1 million excess Federal deposit funds. A Dallas bank makes the best offer and the $1 million is credited to its account with the Fed. In a transaction between the Denver bank's terminal and the Denver Fed's computer, the message is forwarded through the Kansas City Federal Reserve Bank switch to the main switch at Culpeper, Va.—and on through the Dallas Fed switch to the destination bank in Dallas, where it is printed out on the bank's terminal.

The potential impact of this new payments arrangement in terms of customer convenience, marketability, and inter-institutional competition was quickly recognized and it spread rapidly throughout Massachusetts and into New Hampshire. The critical element in the success of the NOW account program appears to have been the elimination of check charges and the consequent intensive promotion of the "no-charge interest paying checking account."

For example, one close observer of the effectiveness of NOW account marketing summarized its impact in Massachusetts for the first nine months of 1974:[17]

Advertising and promotion have created a high consumer awareness of NOW accounts—83% of our survey respondents have heard of it; and awareness reaches the 90% level among young consumers (those between 25-34) and consumers with an annual income higher than $15,000.

By the end of September, some 218,000 NOW accounts were in use, amounting to nearly $228 million in deposits. This is an increase of 145% from the 89,000 accounts in use last December, and an increase of 78% in the $138 million in balances at that time.

By September, the number of NOW accounts in Massachusetts was approximately equal to 13% of the total number of personal-checking accounts. If this trend continues, there probably will be as many as 300,000 accounts by year end for a 19% market penetration. In other words, there would be one NOW account for every five checking accounts in just one year—against a checking account base built up over decades.

The number of banks offering NOW accounts has nearly tripled in the past nine months, and the increase has come in all institutions: mutual savings banks, commercial banks, S&L's, and Coops.

The number of NOW drafts per active account grew about 25% in the first six months and has held steady since then. By September, nearly 23% of NOW customers were writing more than 10 drafts per month, clearly equivalent to checking account usage.

There is increased price competition; 54% of NOW banks in Massachusetts offer free NOWs, and the percent grows monthly at an accelerated rate.

And just to rub it in, 88% of the NOW accounts with 85% of the dollar outstandings were in mutual savings banks, Coops and S&Ls at the end of September. As you may know, the thrift institutions already have a preponderant share of all consumer deposits in Massachusetts.

The above words, of course, speak for themselves. And in response to the success of these thrift institutions commercial banking organizations sought to curtail the spread of NOW accounts through both legislative and regulatory actions.[18] As a result of that pressure, the issuance of NOW accounts has been limited to Massachusetts and New Hampshire by the August 16, 1973 signing of Public Law 93-100 (H.R. 6370) which in Section 2(a) states that "No depository institution shall allow the owner of a deposit or account on which interest or dividends are paid to make withdrawals by negotiable or transferable instruments for the purpose of making transfers to third parties, except that such withdrawals may be made in the States of Massachusetts and New Hampshire." In addition, the Federal Reserve Board, the Federal Deposit Insurance Corporation, and the Federal Home Loan Bank Board adopted regulations to govern NOW account activities in Massachusetts and New Hampshire effective January 1, 1974.[19]

The Payment Order Account. A number of variations on the theme of the NOW account have been introduced and tested in recent months by thrift institutions seeking to move into direct competition with commercial banks in the area of third party payments without technically violating Public Law 93-100.

The mutual savings banks of New York, for example, have introduced their own type of non-interest-bearing statement accounts which allow their customers to write negotiable orders of withdrawal for third party payments. These payment order (POW) accounts both resemble and clear as do ordinary checks.[20] Likewise, the Western Savings Fund Society of Philadelphia initiated its Western Order of Withdrawal (WOW) account program in September, 1974. In this case depositors can write an "unlimited number of payment orders" on their regular savings account provided that they have a minimum balance of $200. But a savings bank official must first receive and sign the order before it becomes valid.[21]

In Connecticut, the Suffield Savings Bank has introduced its "Money-Mate" plan which provides for "personalized checks" to be "drawn against pre-arranged lines of credit" at the savings bank. The checks are then cleared through the normal channels of the commercial banking system.[22]

23

Credit unions are also moving into the third party payments area by means of their "share-draft" or "deposit-draft" systems. In essence, the latter "enable the credit union member to draw on his account without visiting the credit union. With them, he can pay bills by mail and pay for goods and services at the point of purchase."[23]

In point of fact, all of these payment order account experiments, whether currently operating in an EFTS mode or not, are vehicles by means of which thrift institutions intend to participate in the offering of third party payments, the establishment of customer lines of credit, and ultimately the offering of a wide range of consumer-oriented financial services in competition with commercial banks.

The Transmatic Money System. A now famous experiment in the application of electronic funds transfer technology by a thrift institution was undertaken in January, 1974, by the First Federal Savings and Loan of Lincoln, Nebraska. Initially, the Transmatic Money System (TMS), consisted of the installation of computer terminals in just two supermarkets of the Hinky Dinky chain to allow individuals to make remote deposits or withdrawals from their savings accounts.[24]

A typical TMS teller transaction involving the deposit of a portion of an individual's payroll check, for example, would be:

1. The customer brings his check to the most convenient terminal-equipped market, presents a plastic identification card, and directs the market's clerk as to the amounts to be deposited and kept in cash.
2. The terminal captures the relevant customer and deposit-amount information and automatically credits the depositor's account accordingly.
3. The market clerk gives the customer the cash difference between the payroll check and the amount deposited.
4. The market's cash payout to the customer is automatically compensated for by a credit to the market's account with the TMS institution.

First Federal's TMS program was designed to capitalize on the long established consumer habit of cashing checks at supermarkets in order to forge a new relationship involving both retail consumers and

24

Table 2-2

WHERE AND HOW THRIFT INSTITUTIONS ARE MOVING INTO THIRD-PARTY PAYMENT PLANS

State	Check-like-accounts	NOW or WOW	Other payments from savings	Pre-arranged lines of credit	Telephone transfer Account
Alabama				CU	
Alaska				CU	
Arkansas					S&L
California			CU		
Connecticut	MSB*/S&L*		MSB	MSB	
Delaware	MSB				S&L
District of Columbia				CU	S&L
Florida				CU	S&L
Georgia			CU	CU	
Hawaii				CU	
Idaho				CU	
Illinois				CU	S&L
Indiana	MSB			CU	S&L
Kansas				CU	
Louisiana					S&L
Maryland	MSB			CU	S&L
Massachusetts		MSB/S&L		MSB	
Michigan			CU	CU	
Minnesota			CU/MSB*	CU	S&L
New Hampshire		MSB/S&L			
New Jersey	MSB				
New York	MSB		MSB	CU	S&L
North Carolina	CU				
Ohio				CU	
Oklahoma				CU	S&L
Oregon	MSB			CU	
Pennsylvania			MSB	CU	
Rhode Island	CU/MSB/S&L				
South Carolina				CU	S&L
Tennessee				CU	
Texas				CU	S&L
Utah*	CU				S&L
Virginia			S&L		
Washington			S&L	CU	
Wisconsin			CU	CU	

* Not effective yet.

NOTE: This table is not to catalog every thrift institution third-party payment plan but simply to illustrate the scope of a nationwide trend.

KEY: MSB-Mutual Savings Banks; S&L-Savings & Loan Assns.; CU-Credit Unions.

Source: *Banking*, December 1974

retail merchants in a mutually beneficial funds transfer arrangement. In brief, the merchant has to "open an account with the S&L and maintain balances large enough to cover Transmatic transactions" so that when "a customer makes a deposit at the Hinky Dinky store, the computer electronically transfers the amount of the deposit from the store's account to the customer's account" and vice versa in the case of a withdrawal.[25]

The Transmatic Money System has been credited with benefiting the financial institution, the participating merchant, and the consumer. The institution gains the opportunity of offering a new service characterized by convenient location, almost unlimited hours of availability, and low cost. The merchant gains the opportunity to offer a new service and, most importantly, to reduce the amount of on-hand cash required to meet payroll check-cashing demands. And finally, the consumer has what amounts to an interest-bearing and highly convenient transactions account.

Like the NOW account program the Transmatic Money System has had dramatic results. According to the Nebraska Bankers Association, the initial 45 day test of TMS was characterized by 3,169 transactions consisting of $644,031 in deposits, $40,605 in withdrawals, and the opening of 672 new accounts. Furthermore, the cost of a TMS transaction was estimated to be about $.05 as opposed to $2.00 per passbook transaction. And finally, First Federal of Lincoln was pursuing arrangements to install TMS in at least 36 Hinky Dinky stores in Nebraska while also expanding the service to include additional retailers as well as financial institutions.[26]

The extremely favorable response to the Hinky Dinky experiment seems to have established the fact that the public will embrace a program of funds transfer which is geographically and procedurally convenient, pays interest on checking-account types of funds, and provides quick access to cash when the latter is needed. Of equal importance, the TMS experiment has precipitated a competitive response in the form of the Nebraska Bankers Association's proposed Nebraska Electronic Transfer System (NETS) for the express purpose of providing "a full range of services made possible by existing electronic technology, including deposits, withdrawals, transfers and credit line advances."

MINTS. The Mutual Institutions National Transfer System is another recent development designed to provide a computerized network for the relay of administrative and payments messages for savings institutions in a manner parallel to that of the Fed and the Bank wire systems.

The primary objective of the MINTS program is to enable the customer of any member institution to utilize the facilities of any other member to make withdrawals, deposits, or third party payments. The initial "access" or "interchange" key to the MINTS network was a standardized and franchised plastic Money Transfer Card which was issued to customers of MINTS members.[27]

More recently, MINTS has established the specifications for a "second-generation" cash access or debit card which is to be called the Cashmate Card and is to be "fully compatible with present day standards and interchange requirements."[28]

MINTS was incorporated in July, 1972, by the National Association of Mutual Savings Banks and has grown from a January, 1973, membership of 22 institutions to a January, 1975, membership of 301 institutions.[29]

The Federal Home Loan Bank Board. It is worth noting that the Federal Home Loan Bank Board has also added to the institutional pressures for a change in the payments mechanism favorable to thrifts. For example, Chairman Thomas R. Bowmar in testimony before the Subcommittee on Bank Supervision and Insurance of the House Committee on Banking and Currency in November, 1973, commented that,

Important developments are occurring in services designed to convert consumer payments to electronic media. These apply both to preauthorization of recurring bill payments as well as one-time transactions at the retail point-of-sale. When these growing new bank services are coupled with what commercial banks now offer—such as consolidated monthly financial statements showing the depositor the status of his checking, savings, mortgage loan, and consumer loan accounts—savings and loan associations cannot expect to compete effectively and attract an appropriate share of deposit funds, unless they can offer similar services.

Indeed, the FHLBB in mid-1974 proceeded to issue temporary regulations which permit federally chartered savings and loans to set up one or more "remote service units," known as RSUs, which could be located anywhere in the state containing the institution's home office or outside of the state if such a location is still in the primary service area of any branch office of the institution located outside of the state.[30]

According to the FHLBB's regulations, the permissible functions of the remote service units would be to accommodate customer deposits, withdrawals, and loan payments; while the permissible locations for such units would include retail establishments, office buildings, shopping centers, factories, and transportation terminals.[31]

The aggressive posture of the FHLBB with respect to EFTS and savings and loan associations, in the words of one observer, "has made clear its determination to give savings and loan associations every opportunity to develop maximum capability in electronic funds transfer."[32]

Direct Deposit Programs

The latest and perhaps the most significant payments innovations of substantial scale are the already-commenced direct deposit programs for both recurring federal benefits and federal payroll disbursements. The Department of the Treasury and the Federal Reserve System have been in the forefront of designing and implementing these new payments programs.

Recurring Federal Benefits. The motivation for Treasury's undertaking a direct deposit program for recurring federal benefit payments is evident if the costs of a paper transfer system and the quantity and dollar value of routine monthly Treasury disbursements are considered.

For example, Table 2-3 shows the estimated quantity and dollar value of recurring monthly benefit payments.[33]

The legal authority to make a start towards the automation of recurring benefits was derived from Public Law 92-366 (31 U.S.C.A. 492(d) as amended August 7, 1972) which provides "for the making of a payment . . . in favor of a financial institution . . . (for) recurring payments, upon the written request of the person to whom the payment is to be made." In essence, the Government was authorized to make recurring federal benefit payments directly to financial organizations at the request of the beneficiary, and for purposes of the direct deposit program a financial organization was defined as "any bank, savings bank, savings and loan or other similar institution or federal or state chartered credit union."

Table 2-3

MONTHLY VOLUMES AND DOLLAR VALUE

Regular Social Security	28,000,000	$5,068,000,000
Supplemental Security Income	4,500,000	510,000,000
Veterans	6,400,000	870,000,000
Civil Service	1,350,000	433,350,000
Railroad Retirement	1,100,000	220,000,000
Employee Salary	2,000,000	674,355,000
Public Debt Interest	325,000	31,000,000
Totals	43,675,000	$7,806,705,000

Source: Department of the Treasury

Once given the authority to proceed with a program the Treasury and the Social Security Administration "immediately joined in a study to determine the level of interest of financial organizations and beneficiaries in a direct deposit program and to identify and solve problems associated with such a program."[34] Subsequent to the results of their studies the Treasury Department and the Social Security Administration reached an agreement to implement a "Direct Deposit—Electronic Funds Transfer Program" in several phases for both regular social security and supplemental security income payments.

The program being undertaken by the Treasury in cooperation with SSA has formalized three major objectives:[35]

1. To improve service to beneficiaries by eliminating the loss, theft, and forgery, as well as cashing problems of checks.
2. To realize cost reductions and increased efficiency throughout the

29

benefit payments issue and transfer system to the benefit of the operations and customer relations of the financial community.

3. To realize cost reductions in the issuing and clearing of checks for the Government.

In April, 1974, the Treasury and SSA decided upon a three-phase plan for implementing the Direct Deposit Program.

Phase I, which started in Georgia in November, 1974, involved advising social security beneficiaries of the option of routing their monthly payment benefits directly to the financial organization of their choice. Individual checks are still issued in favor of the beneficiary but by means of the Power of Attorney Standard Form 1199 such checks can be directly routed to a specified financial organization. In April, 1975, the direct deposit option was brought to the attention of beneficiaries in Florida (where there are an estimated 1.5 million social security and supplemental income security beneficiaries as contrasted to only about 700,000 in Georgia). On those occasions when informational inserts accompany the checks, the participating financial organizations are expected to forward them to the beneficiary.[36]

Phase II of the program is expected to bring the direct deposit option to beneficiaries on a nationwide basis during the Summer and Fall of 1975. The only major difference between the Phase I and Phase II stages will consist of using Standard Form 1199 so as to permit individual checks to be issued in favor of the beneficiary's designated financial organization in lieu of the beneficiary himself. But as payee the financial organization must then credit the beneficiary's deposit account. Also, the Social Security Administration will be able to manage communications with beneficiaries directly thereby avoiding the check inserts which now pass through financial intermediaries.[37]

Phase III of the program envisions the distribution or effecting of payments by means of electronic transfer through the Federal Reserve System as fiscal agent of the Treasury. Current planning calls for pilot EFTS projects to be initiated in Georgia and Florida at least by early 1976 with nationwide conversion to EFTS to follow sometime thereafter. According to the Treasury,[38]

In Phase III, it is planned that direct deposit payments will be effected by electronic funds transfer through the Federal Reserve System, as

Table 2-4   DIRECT DEPOSIT OF FEDERAL RECURRING BENEFITS
(Quick Reference Chart)

Phase of implementation	Phase I	Phase II	Phase III
Method of payment	Checks drawn to individual benefici-aries and mailed to financial organizations	Checks drawn to financial organiza-tions for credit to an individual beneficiary's account	Electronic funds transfer (EFT): Credit to a Federal Reserve account for ultimate credit to the accounts of individual beneficiaries
Effective dates	November 1974 until complete conversion to other systems	Conversion to commence in September 1975	Testing to begin in late 1975
Affected area	Beneficiaries residing in Georgia and Florida	Nationwide	
Primary controlling regulations	Treasury Circular No. 21	Treasury Circular No. 1076	Treasury Circular to be developed by September 1975
Method of beneficiary enrollment	Beneficiary completes top half of form SF–1199 and takes or sends form to financial organization. Financial organiza-tion completes bottom half, sends original to SSA district office, returns a copy to beneficiary, and retains a copy.		
Method of transmitting communications from Social Security Admin-istration to beneficiaries	All communications will be mailed to financial organizations for for-warding to beneficiaries. These will include: 1. general information notices, mailed with checks—may be sent with monthly statements. 2. adverse action notices, mailed separately—must be sent to beneficiary immediately.	All communications to be mailed by the Government direct to beneficiaries' home address.	
Claims of nonreceipt	A statement of nonreceipt must be submitted to a Social Security Administration district office.		Prior to the filing of a nonreceipt statement, the financial organization should confirm that all credit entries have been properly posted and balanced by the credit passed by the Federal Reserve Bank.

Source: Department of the Treasury

fiscal agent of the Treasury. Treasury plans to furnish payment records on magnetic tape to Federal Reserve Banks, which will in turn make payment from the Treasurer's account by crediting the reserve accounts of member banks with the total amount of payments to them or their correspondent nonmember financial organizations. The Federal Reserve Bank will provide individual records in paper, card or electronic form, as required by the receiving financial organization, for use in posting beneficiaries' accounts.

At present, the Department of the Treasury issues about 43 million recurring checks of which some 32 million are social security and supplemental income security benefits. By progressively expanding the direct deposit program to veterans, civil service, railroad retirement and other recurring payments, the Treasury hopes to put about 40 percent of its current check volume in an EFTS mode by early 1980.

Payroll Deposit. In September, 1973, the United States Air Force and the Federal Reserve System established a test program for the simulation of the payment and distribution of 20,000 payroll deposits. The simulation being successful, was followed-up with an expanded test program in the Fall of 1974. This test consisted of verifying, again by simulation, payroll deposits at financial organizations in California, Georgia, Colorado, Wyoming and a part of New Mexico.

As a result of the success of the simulation tests the Air Force, in cooperation with the Treasury and the Federal Reserve, set up a three-phase program to implement direct payroll deposit on a nationwide basis by early 1976. The first phase began with the electronic distribution of the November 30, 1974, payroll of participants in the Air Force's "Checks to Financial Institutions" program in substitution of the previous mail distribution.[39]

The second phase of the program expanded direct deposit to the remaining areas served by the San Francisco and Atlanta Federal Reserve Districts during the first quarter of 1975; and the final phase will bring the payroll project nationwide by early 1976.[40]

The payments to financial organizations in California and Georgia are being routed through the recently established automated clearing houses, or ACHs, of those states. The distribution of payroll payments to accounts in Colorado, New Mexico, and Wyoming, none of which

FORCES OF TRANSITION

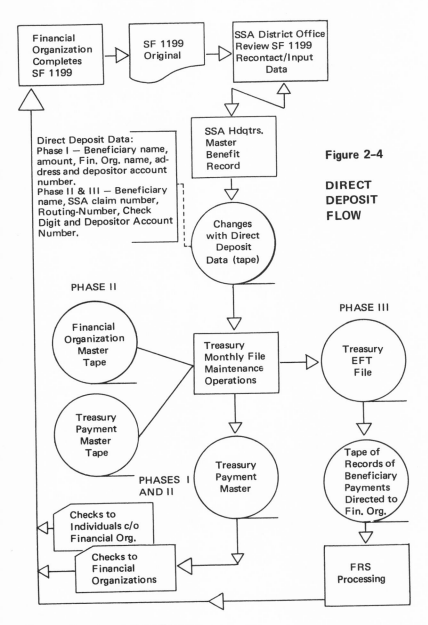

Figure 2–4

DIRECT
DEPOSIT
FLOW

Financial
Organization
Completes
SF 1199

SF 1199
Original

SSA District Office
Review SF 1199
Recontact/Input
Data

Direct Deposit Data:
Phase I — Beneficiary name,
amount, Fin. Org. name, ad-
dress and depositor account
number.
Phase II & III — Beneficiary
name, SSA claim number,
Routing-Number, Check
Digit and Depositor Account
Number.

SSA Hdqtrs.
Master
Benefit
Record

Changes
with Direct
Deposit
Data (tape)

PHASE II

Financial
Organization
Master
Tape

Treasury
Payment
Master
Tape

PHASE III

Treasury
Monthly File
Maintenance
Operations

Treasury
EFT
File

PHASES I
AND II

Treasury
Payment
Master

Tape of
Records of
Beneficiary
Payments
Directed to
Fin. Org.

Checks to
Individuals c/o
Financial Org.

Checks to
Financial
Organizations

FRS
Processing

Source: Department of the Treasury

has a currently operative automated clearing house, is being cleared through the Denver Branch of the Federal Reserve Bank of Kansas City. The Air Force Accounting and Finance Center in Denver delivers the

Table 2–5

AIR FORCE PAYROLL PROJECT

States	No. of Payments	No. of Banks[a]	No. of Thrifts[a]	% of Payments on Tapes & Cards[b]
Georgia				
November, 1974	4,717	244	3	8.0
December, 1974	9,129	241	3	5.5
January, 1975	9,189	241	3	4.0
State Total	23,035			
California				
November, 1974	29,612	57	9	85.0
December, 1974	57,666	93	10	87.0
January, 1975	58,263	95	10	86.5
State Total	145,541			
Colorado, Wyoming, New Mexico				
November, 1974	16,462	255	8	88.0
December, 1974	30,554	258	9	88.0
January, 1975	30,458	258	9	88.0
State Total	77,474			
Grand Total as of January, 1975	246,050			

a. Maximum number participating during month.
b. Average of mid-month and end-of-month payments.
  Source: Federal Reserve Board

payroll records on magnetic tape to the Denver Fed which sorts the account items by computer. Federal reserve couriers take the items for

Figure 2–5

FEDERAL RESERVE
EFT FLOW – TREASURY PAYMENTS

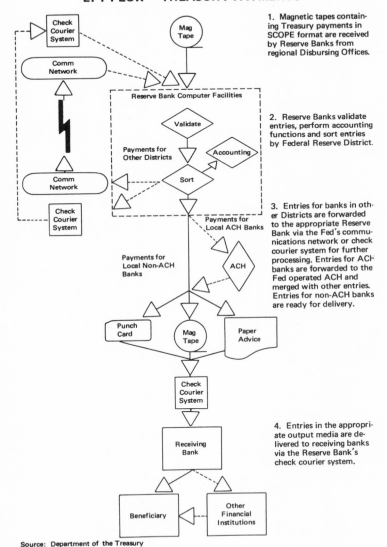

1. Magnetic tapes containing Treasury payments in SCOPE format are received by Reserve Banks from regional Disbursing Offices.

2. Reserve Banks validate entries, perform accounting functions and sort entries by Federal Reserve District.

3. Entries for banks in other Districts are forwarded to the appropriate Reserve Bank via the Fed's communications network or check courier system for further processing. Entries for ACH banks are forwarded to the Fed operated ACH and merged with other entries. Entries for non-ACH banks are ready for delivery.

4. Entries in the appropriate output media are delivered to receiving banks via the Reserve Bank's check courier system.

Source: Department of the Treasury

35

accounts in California and Georgia to the San Francisco and the Atlanta ACHs for distribution.[41]

The Air Force is planning to expand electronic distribution for payroll deposits as rapidly as possible to all Federal Reserve Districts and to all 200,000 Air Force personnel participating in the Checks to Financial Institutions program as of year-end 1974.

CHAPTER 3

BASIC ELEMENTS OF AN E F T S

In October, 1974, the Congress of the United States provided for the creation of a National Commission on Electronic Fund Transfers and in so doing appears to have at least formalized the generic name of the payments mechanism of the future toward which the country is now moving. And while EFTS still means many things to many people it is nevertheless true that a consensus is beginning to develop regarding the basic structure of the prospective electronic payments mechanism.

EFTS Defined

In a very narrow sense EFTS can be thought of as nothing other than an operations-oriented modification in the transfer of funds from one locale to another. In short, it can be viewed as a transfer system in which paper is simply replaced by electronic impulses, the latter being a type of "third generation of money" subsequent to coin/currency and then checks.[1] Within this conceptual framework electronic funds transfer is "simply a tool, but not a product: it provides a superior way to communicate and transport data, consolidate information, and provide customers with direct and discretionary access to financial transactions and records."[2]

To most observers and proposed participants, however, EFTS has come to embrace not only the narrow or literal electronic transfer function itself but rather a wide range of new service and convenience elements. For example, one expert has defined EFTS in its broadest sense as embracing all of the following elements:[3]

1. The electronic transfer of funds between corporations and banks nationally either on a direct basis or through the Federal Reserve System.
2. The automation of preauthorized debit or credit payments for individuals and enterprises in which automated clearing houses (ACHs) would be the focal point for the handling, clearing, and settlement functions among banks and the Federal Reserve.
3. The authorization for and the execution of both cash and credit exchanges of value on either an immediate or a delayed basis as determined at the point of sale. Both thrift and demand deposit accounts would be used for third party transfers.
4. The provision of a comprehensive range of financial services for both individuals and organizations at points of convenient location. Such services would include cash deposit and withdrawal; the transfer of funds between accounts; budget management services; and so on.
5. The establishment of national, local, and regional electronic clearing facilities for effecting all of the above.

Generally speaking, most of the basic elements of the prospective electronic funds transfer system can be classified as having (1) clearing network characteristics, (2) remote service or point of sale characteristics, and (3) preauthorized debit and/or credit characteristics.[4] Also, there is general agreement that the final form or design of our electronic payments mechanism will be that design which simultaneously satisfies the major needs and requirements of consumers, commercial customers, financial organizations, and government regulators. Whether or not this implies but one public utility type of system or several proprietary systems is not yet clear.

The Automated Clearing House

Perhaps the most fundamental element of an electronics-oriented payments mechanism is the automated clearing house, commonly known as an ACH. In its most simple form the ACH represents the electronic counterpart of a standard check-clearing facility which is established and operated on behalf of local or regional associations of commercial banks. In this case the data that is normally captured and processed from checks is replaced by a system in which magnetic tapes are used for the computer-based capture and transfer of the necessary administrative and payments information between participating financial institutions.[5] In short, the simple ACH replaces check-clearing facilities with paperless-entry facilities which clear by means of electronic impulse (dubbed "blip and bleep" clearing).

The Federal Reserve Board, while discussing the purposes and functions of the Federal Reserve System, has alluded to the automated clearing house in its most basic capacity as follows:[6]

The expense and complexity of processing and transporting the enormous volume of paper checks has prompted the banking industry to begin the establishment of a paperless electronic means of transferring funds. The formation of automated clearing houses (ACHs) is one method that is being used to transfer funds without requiring paper checks. These ACHs make possible the exchange of payments—such as for payrolls and dividends—through electronically processable media. The ACH computer processes the transfers, and these are delivered to recipient banks for posting to customer accounts.

In the more comprehensive and more commonly understood sense, however, the ACH has come to represent the focal point for a wide range of electronically-implemented financial services for both consumer and commercial customers. For example, the nation's first ACH, which became operational in California in late 1972, constitutes a system "designed to replace checks as a mechanism for the making of mortgage, insurance, utility and other regularly recurring payments by consumers" while also providing for the automation of "wage, dividend, and other recurring payments to consumers."[7]

Legally speaking, the California Automated Clearing House (CACH) requires but a single document or authorization by the depositor "which by its terms remains effective until revoked by the depositor or cancelled by his bank" before undertaking the automatic transfer of funds into or out of the depositor's demand account.[8]

R. R. Campbell, writing in the July, 1974, issue of the "FHLBB Journal," described the services and operations of the New England

Automated Clearing House (NEACH) as follows:[9]

Specifically, the New England Automated Clearing House offers direct deposit of payroll to S&L customers' accounts, and deposit of social security income, VA payments and dividends, corporation and insurance company dividends and annuities.

NEACH also offers a service to account-holders for bill paying by preauthorized fixed debits; i.e., mortgage payments, automatic savings deposits, insurance premium payments, level-payment utility bills, installment loan payments and contractual payments.

Finally, it offers a variable debit service through the bill check procedure which allows the customer to preapprove department store bills for automated debit, as well as credit card bills, bank card bills, and regular utility bills.

The addition of these services, with a single descriptive statement, can give the average family an opportunity to place a good part of its financial transactions, and the accounting for them, with its savings and loan association.

Where NOW accounts also are offered, the average family can get the whole package of family financial services, except personal loans, from its savings and loan association.

NEACH receives inputs from originating banks. It sorts and sends them out automatically to receiving banks and, as a by-product, provides the information needed to settle accounts between originators and receivers, either directly or through their correspondents who are members of the Federal Reserve System.

The procedures are akin to and hardly more complex than those relating to the paper payments system for clearing NOW accounts. The Automated Clearing House takes the place of present paper clearing house procedures. The relationships with the Federal Reserve and correspondent banks for clearing accounts are substantially the same as for NOW accounts, as are those with service bureaus for handling customer account detail.

The ACH movement originated in California in 1968 when about ten California banks formed a Special Committee on Paperless Entries, known as SCOPE, to develop the technical, legal, and operational structure for a "preauthorized paperless entry" transfer mechanism.[10] The hardware and software system developed by SCOPE was subsequently copied by the Atlanta Committee on Paperless Entry, or COPE, on behalf of the Georgia Automated Clearing House Association. Automated clearing house facilities modeled on the original SCOPE system were operating as of December, 1974, in San Francisco,

Los Angeles, Atlanta, Boston, and Minneapolis/St. Paul with numerous others being organized. To accommodate and facilitate the ACH movement the National Automated Clearing House Association (NACHA) was formed in mid-1974 with 18 charter member regional associations representing population centers in all 12 Federal Reserve Districts.[11]

Some of the reasons advanced to explain the relatively early success of the ACH systems are that (1) the problems of technology are minimal; (2) the initial investment is relatively low and can be spread out among a number of institutions; (3) the ACH movement is strongly supported by the Federal Reserve System; and (4) the ACH systems have potential large volume utilization (e.g., the direct deposit programs for federal recurring benefits and payrolls).[12]

Finally, it is worth noting that just as the locally oriented ACH movement is complementing the national Fed Wire and Bank Wire clearing networks the newly formed Society for Worldwide Interbank Financial Telecommunications (SWIFT) is going to enable user banks to transmit international payments, statements, and other banking messages among themselves in an electronic mode.[13]

The Automated Teller Machine

While the ACH movement was getting underway in the late 1960s and early 1970s as a cooperative and risk-sharing enterprise, the commercial banking community was simultaneously putting into place networks of proprietary and competitive remote service units, also known as customer bank communication terminals or CBCTs. The latter have been evolving from the form of standard branch banks to combinations of bank offices and cash dispensing machines and more recently to the free-standing and remotely-located automated teller machine (ATM).[14]

The comprehensive ATM is generally capable of providing a bank customer practically any service available from a standard teller-operated office including cash withdrawals from savings or checking accounts; cash deposits; inter-account funds transfer; withdrawals charged against credit cards; and bill payments by account-debiting. And all of the latter can be executed at less cost per transaction and greatly increased customer convenience in terms of time and location.[15] The Transmatic Money System discussed previously, and now finding widespread imitation, was really little more than the adoption of a simple ATM concept by a thrift institution.

The widespread public acceptance of automated banking facilities is evidenced by rapid growth of ATM installations. For example, in 1969 there were but an estimated two fully operational ATM facilities in the United States whereas there are currently in excess of 2,200 such facilities in operation, with an estimated potential of some 35,000 by 1980.[16]

The impact of the trend toward ATM facilities has been most evident to date on two areas of banking: (1) in the data processing and operations techniques utilized; and (2) in the actual bank building facilities themselves. In the first case, ATM facilities are requiring banks to issue cards to all customers instead of to just credit worthy customers; to convert from batch to on-line computer processing; to consider comprehensive bank communication systems accessed by remote service units; and to convert from passbook types of accounts to periodic statement types of accounts. In the second case, banking facilities are becoming grouped as stand-alone automated facilities without branch office potential; as structures with in-lobby ATMs and branch office potential; and as combination live and automated teller facilities.[17]

Although the ATM is not conducive to financial transactions requiring the personal judgment of management and for the most part is not capable of taking on new customers, the fact remains that ATM facilities currently offer good alternatives to extended banking hours, physical expansion, and increasing personnel requirements and costs. And given recent liberalizing regulations by both the Federal Home Loan Bank Board and the Office of the Comptroller of the Currency regarding thrift institution and commercial bank installation of remote service units, the utilization of automated teller machines can be expected to accelerate rapidly.

The Point of Sale Terminal

The automated teller machine discussed above is often viewed as representing the first generation of remote service units. In a sense, the ATM merely extends, in terms of location and convenience, the already existing two-party relationship between a customer and his financial institution. However, the single most important factor in the ultimate success or failure of a universal electronic funds transfer system appears to be the point of sale (POS) terminal.[18] The POS terminal can be viewed as a second-generation remote service unit which is capable of electronically placing a third party into the customer-financial institution communication's link.

In a generic sense the POS terminal includes check verification terminals, credit authorization terminals, cash deposit and cash withdrawal terminals, and the cash sale or third party payment terminal.[19]

A check verification terminal would be used at the point of sale to determine whether the customer has sufficient funds in his account to cover his purchase. The credit authorization terminal would simply permit the retailer to obtain an on-line authorization of the customer's proposed card or check credit purchase from that customer's financial institution. But in neither case do these arrangements fundamentally alter already-existing payments methods.

Cash deposit and withdrawal terminals are also more associated with the convenience aspects of EFTS than with any real change in the payments system itself. This is not to suggest, however, that these types of terminal arrangements—comparable to ATMs—are inconsequential, as was proven in the Lincoln, Nebraska, experiment in the Hinky Dinky supermarkets.

The widespread introduction of cash point of sale terminals, however, would represent a basic change in our payments mechanism. The traditional paper flows would be replaced by on-line electronic messages involving the instantaneous verification of accounts and the transfers of funds from customers to merchants, debiting the former and crediting the latter at the exact same financial organization or, through complex computer switching centers, at geographically distant financial organizations.

In time, a single POS terminal can be expected to handle all of

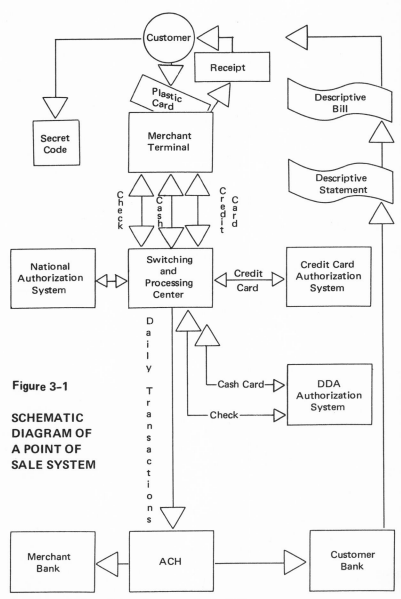

Figure 3-1

SCHEMATIC DIAGRAM OF A POINT OF SALE SYSTEM

Source: L. Richard Fisher, *Consumer Credit 1975*, Practising Law Institute, p. 268.

the above types of terminal-oriented transactions upon being accessed by a customer card. And since the POS terminal would be the real interface between the public and the payments mechanism, its widespread acceptance and use are considered the key to the needed volume and economic viability required for achieving a true electronic funds transfer system.

Pilot projects involving limited function POS terminals have already been carried out. For example, the Syosset Branch of the Hempstead Bank on Long Island started a fourteen month experiment in November, 1971. Customers were issued uniquely coded cards and terminals were installed in 35 stores. When making a purchase the customer's card was entered into the terminal, the customer then keyed in his own secret security code, and upon automated approval, the customer's account would be electronically debited and the merchant's account credited.[20]

A second POS terminal experiment was undertaken in Upper Arlington, Ohio, a suburb of Columbus, by the City National Bank of Columbus during 1971 and 1972. Limited function POS terminals were used in this program to obtain credit authorizations and to capture the customer and merchant data required to complete all credit card transactions. Such data were stored during the day on magnetic tape and then the account of the merchant was credited each evening as indicated by that data.[21]

The reader should realize, however, that many of the pilot projects in electronic funds transfer have rapidly taken on the look of both large scale and permanence. This has certainly been the case with the direct deposit programs discussed previously and is now becoming the case in POS systems.

For example, in late 1973, the First National City Bank of New York issued a terminal readable "Citicard" to some 800,000 personal checking account customers as well as a terminal readable credit card to about 920,000 Master Charge customers primarily for credit authorization purposes.[22] By the Summer of 1974, FNCB had "launched an on-line check authorization service" for its Citicard holders which allowed them "to use or cash personal checks at merchant locations without regular identification procedures."[23] And while "check transactions on the Citicard do not result in an immediate transfer of funds," as would be the case in a true EFTS system, still "a debit memo is automatically posted to the account."[24]

It is interesting to note that by the end of 1974, FNCB was reporting the installation of 6,000 terminals evenly divided between merchants and branches. Furthermore, Master Charge credit authorizations were averaging "better than 20,000 per day" while some "1.1 million Citicards generate an average of 200,000 transactions per day."[25]

The one POS system to date which appears to be a true EFTS system, that is, automatically debiting the customer's account and crediting the merchant's account, is the Instant Transaction system developed, tested, and recently patented by the Hempstead Bank of Long Island, New York.[26]

Preauthorized Credits and Debits

The preauthorized payment of payrolls (credits) and bills (debits) of individuals, corporations and governments is already taking place in scattered instances with our present check-based system and this type of service appears to be a major element of a prospective electronic funds transfer system, especially in conjunction with other ACH services.[27]

In general, automated payroll depositing requires the disbursing company, agency or institution to create a computer tape on which the payee's bank number, bank account, and amount to be credited have been captured. Then at some time before the required payment date the tape is forwarded to the company's bank for screening. Any amounts to be credited to accounts at that bank are removed and the tape is then forwarded to an ACH for further screening, sorting out of financial organizations, and finally the transfer of the specified payment amounts. The respective financial organizations then credit the accounts of the employer's payees on the normal payday.[28]

Those financial organizations unable to receive electronic credits would instead receive a standard printed statement carrying the necessary customer and amount information. Payees receive a printed record of their receipts on their usual bank statement.

Hypothetically speaking, direct deposit plans should be attractive to payees for reasons of payment security and convenience, while the disbursing institution would benefit from decreased check writing and handling costs, more rapid reconciliation of company accounts and protection against fraud.

A variation on the theme of preauthorized payments to the accounts of individuals or corporations is the preauthorized or automatic debiting of such accounts. This too is nothing new to the exchange system but it has been implemented rather randomly and on a small scale. But since an estimated 40 percent or so of the checks

Figure 3–2

PREAUTHORIZED CREDIT

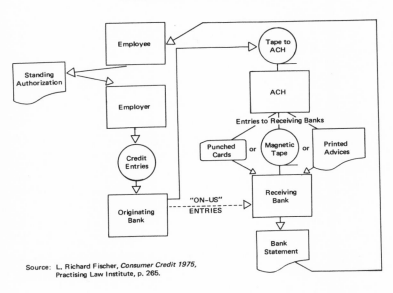

Source: L. Richard Fischer, *Consumer Credit 1975,* Practising Law Institute, p. 265.

written by individuals are for the purpose of making payments to retailers, utilities, and credit card companies, the prospect is for a sizable impact on check volume as a result of an electronic preauthorized debit system.[29]

In general, the preauthorized debit system would reverse the flow of information and payment associated with the credit approach discussed earlier. For example, the customer would preauthorize his financial organization to pay any bills submitted by specified

EFTS

companies. The company would then create a computer tape listing of all the individuals enrolled in its preauthorized debit program along with the amounts to be debited from such participants' accounts, the account number, the number of the financial organization, and the due date for the payment. The tape is forwarded to the company's bank first for screening and then to an ACH for the relay of the remaining administrative and payments transfer data.[30]

Figure 3-3

PREAUTHORIZED DEBIT

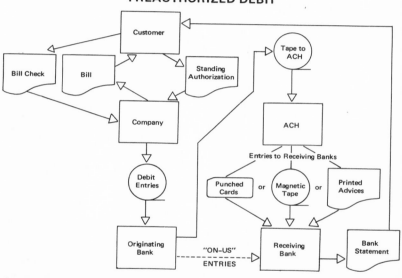

Source: L. Richard Fischer, *Consumer Credit 1975,* Practising Law Institute, p. 264.

Pilot projects for both preauthorized credits and debits have been undertaken. The direct deposit programs for federal recurring benefits and payrolls are the most comprehensive tests to date of the preauthorized credit concept. The preauthorization of debits is currently undergoing volume testing by the Equitable Life Assurance Society which became the first multi-region user of ACH facilities for preauthorized insurance payment entries. In September, 1974, Equitable was processing 27,000 entries per month by magnetic tape and projected a potential volume of 87,000 entries a month.[31] But at the

48

same time the "Bill Check" program of automatic debits in Atlanta, Georgia, was encountering some resistance on the part of consumers and businesses both of whom appeared to be skeptical of its benefits to them.

The Customer Card

In a very real sense the foundation for an electronic payments mechanism is already in place. Most of the elements of such a system exist and are familiar to a large number of financial organizations. But the interconnection of these elements in such a manner as to form an efficient and widely accepted national automated payments network remains to be agreed upon and implemented.

Since most financial transactions involve different degrees of complexity it can reasonably be expected that an EFTS system will be set up in steps that accommodate the simple types of transactions first and then build toward accommodating the more complex transactions. For example, interbusiness transactions often involve a wide range of information—account numbers, department numbers, model numbers, payment dates, invoice numbers, delivery points, and so on—that does not lend itself to near-term EFTS adaptation.

Transactions between individuals or between individuals and business institutions are generally the least complex and for that reason the first steps toward EFTS are likely to revolve around gaining convenient consumer access to that system. To this date the most significant new method of directly interfacing the consumer with the payments mechanism has been by means of the plastic coded card. Indeed, single- or multiple-source plastic coded cards would appear to be the most probable means of popular access to EFTS.[32]

Bank Credit Cards. In spite of a relatively short history the growth of bank credit card use has been nothing short of phenomenal. For example, in 1967, bank credit card year-end outstandings amounted to $0.8 billion while in 1973 those year-end outstandings had grown to $6.6 billion. And bank credit card volume in 1973 had reached about $13.5 billion.[33] Furthermore, Federal Reserve survey data have shown that some 6 of every 10 commercial banks provided credit card services at the end of 1972 and also that most of these banks belong to one or both of the major bank credit card associations.[34]

The reasons generally offered for the widespread consumer acceptance and utilization of bank cards include: (1) the user is assured of the ability to make payments without inconvenience on a nationwide basis; (2) a single customer-bank arrangement provides for practically any type of customer transaction; (3) the customer's personal account records are made available in convenient form and time; (4) the customer does not need large cash balances on his person; and (5) the customer largely controls the cost of the card plan by his own payment preferences.[35]

Experience with bank credit card plans has established that profitability requires (1) a large number of cardholders and (2) a numerous and "varied merchant membership" in the program area.[36] The need for extensive customer and merchant participation per card program is amply demonstrated by the fact that of a relatively large number of initial bank card plans most have been abandoned in favor of participation in either the BankAmericard or the Master Charge programs.

In general terms, those banks in a given market area which are interested in issuing charge cards will form an association of a nonprofit character for the purpose of handling the paper and payments transfers which arise when participating banks honor one another's charge cards. More specifically, member banks will issue their own cards, sign up their own merchants, monitor their own customer accounts, but still accommodate other bank issued cards by routing the related paper through the association clearing house.[37]

On occasion the customer's bank and the merchant's bank do not belong to the same clearing house association. In this case the merchant's bank forwards the card-imprinted receipt to its own association and receives a discounted payment; the receipt is then forwarded to the association of the customer's bank for another discounted payment; the process then repeats itself with respect to the customer's bank which ultimately collects the face amount of the receipt from the card holder.

In essence, the bank credit card receipt clearing mechanism is a duplication of the Federal Reserve's check clearing system. Since the latter will not accept credit card receipts, the banking system must support separate clearing mechanisms, both of which require a paper transfer for each and every transaction. It is not surprising, therefore, that the major bank card programs are now implementing automated clearing mechanisms similar to the Fed Wire and the Bank Wire. For example, as recently as November 1, 1974, National BankAmericard, Inc. announced that,[38]

As scheduled almost eighteen months ago, NBIs BASE (BankAmericard Service Exchange) II System for electronic draft data transmission now links all 86 BankAmericard processing centers in the U.S., including Alaska and Hawaii, on a computer-to-computer basis. The system is expected to handle between 500,000 and 750,000 interchange items daily during the month of November, a figure that is expected to grow to 1,000,000 by March 1, 1975.

All processing centers now are receiving incoming draft data electronically through the BASE II System. Many centers are likewise transmitting outgoing draft data electronically; centers not presently transmitting will be phased into the system prior to next March 1, by which time all BankAmericard interchange transactions will be processed electronically.

Using BASE II, BankAmericard processing centers no longer separate, sort and mail interchange sales draft paper. Instead, information from that paper is captured on magnetic tape and transmitted daily over telephone lines to a central NBI computer facility which in turn sorts and distributes the data to appropriate card-issuing processing centers. The paper remains at merchant bank processing centers. Interchange is accomplished overnight, thereby eliminating six to eight days from the average draft processing and transit time.

It is estimated that BASE II will save NBI members between $14 million and $17 million in gross clearing costs in the first year of operation.

Another example of the strong emphasis being put on EFTS systems by the major bank card associations is evidenced in some excerpts of an October 2, 1974, speech by John J. Reynolds, President and Chief Executive Officer of Interbank Card Association. For example, Reynolds stated that,

EFT services will include both credit and debit capabilities in connection with personal banking services and these personal banking EFT services will be accessed through a piece of plastic.

The role Interbank should and will play in the emerging EFT environment will be to create new means by which our members can perform electronic funds transfers inexpensively and effectively. And, we hope to foster an atmosphere in which our members can offer such EFT services to their customers as are appropriate in their individual marketplace.

EFT will be the electronic interfacing of local, regional and national systems for the purpose of transferring funds between banks, retailers, small businesses, large corporations and the consumer.

Table 3-1

AMOUNTS OUTSTANDING FOR SELECTED CREDIT PLANS

(millions of dollars)

Type of Plan	Dec. 1967	Dec. 1972
Bank credit card plans	828	5408
Travel/entertainment card credit	61	164
Oil company card credit	939	1762
Retail charge accounts[a]	6041	7055

a. Do not include balances on budget or extended payment accounts.
   Source: Federal Reserve Board

Table 3-2

ESTIMATED CREDIT CARD USE — 1970

Type of Card	Estimated Volume ($billions)
Retail store	25.8
Oil	7.4
Bank	7.0
T&E	5.0
Air travel	1.6
Rent-a-car	1.3
Miscellaneous	10.0
Total	58.1

Source: Arthur D. Little, Inc.

In summary, it can be seen that both major bank card associations view EFTS as a comprehensive network which will electronically interconnect banks, merchants, and consumers. The plastic coded customer card which now interconnects these network elements by initiating paper-based transactions data is seen as the key to the ultimate initiation of electronic impulses throughout that payments network. Finally, the clearinghouse part of the network is already set up and operating electronically while awaiting the ultimate resolution of electronic interfacing with the public through the widespread distribution of card-oriented POS terminals.

Nonbank Cards. In addition to the bank credit card there remains a significant number of nonbank cards issued by such institutions as travel and leisure companies, oil companies, retailers, nonbank financial organizations, and others. A good many of these various card-issuing institutions are making efforts to increase both the volume and the complexity of the transactions which their systems can accommodate. Furthermore, most institutions are intent on keeping a proprietary interest in their own card system when economically feasible.

Debit Cards. Customer cards which have the primary function of effecting third party payments or of otherwise allowing the card holder remote access to his asset accounts, including a savings account or checking account, are becoming commonly known as "debit" cards or "asset" cards. The latter may or may not have a credit extending capability. The formerly discussed Citicard, and its competitor the Convenience Card of Chase Manhattan Bank, are basically of this genre. In addition, both of the major bank credit systems are developing their own versions of POS-oriented debit cards as are numerous other institutions.

Whether it be a card initiated purchase and payment, account verification, credit authorization, cash deposit, cash withdrawal, preauthorization, or other transfer of funds it appears that for the near future at least the technology for public participation in EFTS will be based on the plastic coded customer card.

CHAPTER 4

UNRESOLVED ISSUES

It was stated at the outset of this study of EFTS that every major change in the exchange mechanism was associated with an alteration in the balance of power of the various sectors of economic society. And the advent of electronic funds transfer systems in substitution of our current payments mechanism also seems destined to bring about some radical changes, many of which are as yet unforeseen, in both our institutional and social relationships. Already one observer of the EFTS phenomenon has commented that, "These changes proceed from radical advances in technology comparable to those of the Industrial Revolution—but in fact they are even more revolutionary because they are occurring far more rapidly."[1]

In the abstract, the EFTS problem is one of whether new computer and communication technologies, as applied to the exchange mechanism, will result in systematic and beneficial changes or random and detrimental changes. Practically speaking, there are as many issues to be resolved as there are groups of participants in economic exchange.

It is also quite likely that if the major policy issues fail to receive balanced and objective attention, or if they should be viewed through the distorted lens of self-interest, they will remain unresolved. As a consequence, EFTS development and public acceptance could be significantly slowed. Or, in what could be an even worse situation, EFTS might be implemented in a rapid and random manner to the ultimate detriment of all concerned parties.[2] And the policy issues involved range from that of control of the EFT system to that of the individual's privacy and security within such a system.

The Federal Reserve

As is the case with most technologically-based change, the early stages of EFTS development were concerned with the operational aspects of the technology itself. This changed abruptly, however, when on November 19, 1973, the Federal Reserve Board of Governors published a proposal for the revision of Regulation J and invited comments on that proposal.[3]

Historically, Regulation J has governed only the collection of checks but, according to FRB Governor Mitchell, "The proposed revision suggests a legal framework for electronic funds transfer, both the passing of credit, and the collection of payments."[4] And in recognition of the fact that "the development of electronic funds transfer involves new relationships and roles for various institutions, public and private," the Board invited specific comment on a range of important issues which included:[5]

The appropriate roles in the ownership and operation of an electronic payments system—including adjuncts thereto—of (a) the Federal Reserve System, (b) other public bodies, and (c) individual or groups of private institutions, including commercial banks, automated clearinghouses, credit card companies, thrift institutions, credit unions, the "bank wire," and other institutions or organizations such as those specified in the . . . proposal.

The extent and the conditions of access to the electronic funds transfer system by various kinds of depositor institutions, and of other financial institutions, as well as the terms of access.

How the cost of electronic funds transfer should be allocated, including such questions as whether the Federal Reserve should charge for the use of its facilities; if so, against whom should the charges be levied, whether they should cover all costs, and whether reserves maintained by member banks should be taken into account in any fee schedule which might differentiate between Federal Reserve member and nonmember institutions.

The net effect of the Board's Regulation J proposal was to stimulate the still on-going examination of a wide range of EFTS policy issues. Most of these issues are inextricably related as will become evident in the following discussions.

Payments System Control

The issue of the control of the automated payments mechanism of the future revolves largely around the problem of which economic sector, or sectors, will decide the conditions for the utilization of both the terminal entry points and the communication and clearing network of such a system. More specifically, problems concerning standards ownership, accessibility, and regulation must be resolved in surroundings in which each and every potential EFTS participant will be watching and contesting proposed resolutions in order to protect his own autonomy, competitive ability, and freedom of choice.

Standards. With respect to EFTS standards it must be decided whether all terminal entry points, irrespective of location and ownership, must offer the same range of transaction capabilities, some minimum of such capabilities, or at least some fixed combination of all transaction capabilities. Furthermore, it must be determined whether terminal entry points will be designed to permit accessing by any legal activating device, such as plastic coded cards or "touch-tone" phone, or whether accessing can be restricted to proprietary services and activating devices. The same type of "uniformity-diversity" problem applies to the communication and clearing networks of an automated payments mechanism.

Payments system experience to date has been mixed on the matter of uniformity and diversity. For the most part, diversity has been emphasized across competing systems, while uniformity has been emphasized within given systems.

For example, the Federal Reserve Wire, the Bank Wire, the major bank card service exchanges, and MINTS are all uniquely owned and operated networks which offer differentiated clearing services in competition to each other. However, within those clearing networks a substantial uniformity in hardware, software, and policy matters may be required. Just such an emphasis on system uniformity was evidenced by the unprecedented arrangement by which MINTS contracted to buy both automated teller equipment and cash dispensers from one supplier for its system members—all of whom are otherwise competitors.[7] Regional automated clearing houses are also proprietary in terms of ownership and services offered, although a certain amount of operation and service uniformity is promoted by the NACHA payments model. In what must be considered another effort to achieve greater EFTS standardization, the American Bankers Association in January, 1975, announced its intention to launch a pilot study aimed at developing a prototype model which could be used to guide ABA members and state banking associations in their design of electronic payments systems.[8]

The experience to date on terminal entry points and customer interfacing devices has been almost exclusively that of diverse systems. For example, both major bank card systems have announced their intentions to add proprietary payments services to their current credit services. The Citicard and Convenience Card systems are also proprietary in nature and compete on the basis of service differentiation. The Transmatic Money System of the First Federal of Lincoln, Nebraska, and the Instant Transaction system of the Hempstead Bank are other examples of a growing number of differentiated customer interface systems.

The inevitable conclusion is, that as of yet, and for the foreseeable future, there will be not one standard payments system but rather a multiple of payments systems. In short, the emphasis is still one of plurality in EFTS.

Ownership. The ownership of terminals, clearing networks, and payments processes is perhaps the single most sensitive issue regarding the changeover to EFTS. Obviously, ownership will go a long way toward delineating control, management, maintenance, and liability responsibilities. The questions which have to be answered are: Will each group of competitive financial organizations ultimately own and operate its own terminals, access devices, processes and clearing networks to the exclusion of others? Will participating retailers or merchants have the option of owning their terminals for interconnect with whichever payments system they prefer? Will ownership be restricted to just those establishments which hold direct membership in a given payments system or will some form of "correspondent" or indirect access suffice? And finally, who will be liable for error, equipment failure, fraud, or any other malfunctions of the terminal and clearing systems?[9]

Again, the experience to date has been that of diverse rather than uniform ownership arrangements. The Fed Wire, the Bank Wire, and the bank card networks are uniquely owned and have the express purpose of servicing their respective memberships. ACHs are also uniquely owned and their conditions for access by other institutions have, in fact, differed.[10]

It is interesting to note that the establishment of MINTS was really nothing other than a defensive tactic by mutual savings banks to protect themselves from unfavorable conditions of participation in, or outright exclusion from, clearing networks owned by commercial banks. In a similar defensive maneuver, credit unions have proceeded to develop their own proprietary customer interface devices and clearing networks.[11] In fact, in mid 1974 the Kansas Credit Union League went so far as to purchase a commercial bank with the objective of gaining ownership access to any regional or nationwide electronic transfer networks which the commercial banking system might establish.[12]

The pattern of ownership has been equally erratic in remote service units. In general, commercial banks and thrift institutions have retained exclusive ownership of cash dispensers and automated teller machines irrespective of location. However, there have been some instances of commercial banks and thrift institutions sharing ownership and use of a given remote service unit at a particular location.[13] On the other hand, POS terminals are generally purchased and owned by retailers for the express purpose of interconnecting to a particular payments mechanism, be it their own or that of an outside source.

Accessibility. It should be kept in mind, however, that ready access to the terminals and the clearing networks of the EFT system is a concern which extends far beyond the financial sectors. Disproportionate competitive advantages or disadvantages may very well accrue to different sectors of the economy depending upon their access to EFTS and the terms of that access.

If the desired economies of scale cannot be realized by smaller merchants or in geographic areas, suppliers of terminals and clearing facilities may not be willing to invest in such potential loss locations.

The result would be a competitive disadvantage for the merchants or areas so affected. Likewise, there is the possibility that both individuals and merchants will suffer a form of abrogation of their economic freedoms if they are denied reasonable terms and ready access to the automated payments mechanism for causes determined by the private sponsors of proprietary systems.

The concern of different financial organizations over accessibility to EFT systems is quite obvious. It is now evident that individuals, business entities, and entire communities will show similar concerns about all aspects of EFTS. It may well be, therefore, that the service gaps left by the private sector will have to be filled by publicly sponsored electronic payments systems.

Regulation. All of the problems ultimately lead to the issue of the regulation of the prospective automated payments mechanism. In theory, it must be decided whether or not governmental agencies will assume the responsibilities of comprehensive regulation of the terms and conditions of payments system participation or if such regulation will be left in the hands of private clearing house associations, suppliers of equipment, competing groups of financial organizations, public sector citizens associations, or combinations of these groups.

But practically speaking, it has been observed that our current financial world is a "world of compartments created by law."[14] And these compartments, or groups of specialized financial institutions, are already regulated by numerous Federal and State agencies many of which have assumed aggressive and often conflicting positions on the development and implementation of EFT systems.[15]

While the issue of regulation is still open and subject to vigorous debate it nevertheless seems reasonable to expect that Federal regulation of electronic payments systems will be established in the not-too-distant future. Whether this regulation of the financial sectors of the economy will continue to be shared, as now, by such agencies as the Federal Reserve Board, the Comptroller of the Currency, the Federal Home Loan Bank Board and others, or whether some new and pervasive type of "National Payments Authority" will be authorized is not yet clear. But the undisputed importance of the exchange mechanism to economic society and the revolutionary character of EFTS practically dictates a Federal regulatory role.

The Allocation of Costs

Another critical issue cited by the Board of Governors in its proposed revision of Regulation J, in addition to the issues of ownership and access, was that of the allocation of the costs of an EFT system among its users. Specifically, the Federal Reserve was seeking an answer to how it would levy charges but, in general, the cost allocation problem, like the ownership and access problems, extends to all levels of EFTS participation. There is not yet any agreement as to how the costs of an EFT system should be shared among government, financial institutions, business organizations, and individuals.[16]

A major difficulty in the cost allocation problem is that there has been little or no experience with a comprehensive EFTS. Therefore, the data required for reliable estimates of the costs of electronic payments systems, especially on the national level, do not exist. In addition, no uniform procedure for measuring the costs of now-existing EFT systems has been established and it is really not known whether the consumer, the commercial user or intermediary, or the sponsoring financial institutions absorb the greatest burden.[17]

As a result of cost ignorance many potential users of EFTS are now in the uncomfortable position of having to decide whether to invest in a new payments system with unknown cost factors or to remain with the current check and cash system with which they are familiar although competitively insecure. Certainly, the ultimate procedures for allocating costs among participants in the payments mechanism, and the overall cost of such a mechanism, can have a significant impact on the competitive abilities of different participants, the relative attractiveness of different transfer services, and the ultimate acceptance of EFTS by the public.

As difficult as the cost allocation problem is, one conclusion does appear to be justified: If the Federal Reserve System does assume ownership of the EFT system and if its payments services are not priced at their true cost then the Fed "will render difficult if not impossible the creation of private competitors" with a resulting "distortion of economic costs" and "misallocation of resources in electronic funds transfer facilities."[18]

Cooperation or Competition

The traditional coin, currency, and check payments mechanism is often referred to as a "transparent" or "neutral" mechanism. This means, in essence, that the mechanics of effecting payment confer neither competitive advantages nor disadvantages on system participants and do not seriously impinge upon the establishment of optimal transactions patterns by the various sectors of the economy. For financial institutions this has meant that the products or services offered have historically constituted elements of competition; the "check-technology" of the payments mechanism, on the other hand, has been of a universal nature and in the public domain. In addition, the Federal Reserve System has largely ensured the acceptability and clearing of check payments irrespective of the check-issuing institution or the type and location of transaction.[19]

But the advent of multiple and proprietary EFT systems operating independently of a single dominant clearing and coordinating authority has precipitated a situation in which alternative payments mechanisms, as well as financial services, have become potential elements of competition.[20] This has given rise to the very difficult problem of determining "where the dividing line should be drawn between competition and cooperation in the development, use and offering of electronic money systems."[21]

Since the relative balance of cooperation and competition has significant legal and economic antitrust implications, a vigorous debate has developed on whether the product and the delivery mechanism in an EFTS environment can realistically be differentiated. And if so, then how are the most beneficial boundaries between cooperation and competition to be decided in order to achieve an efficient and publicly accepted automated payments mechanism?

A commonly held view is that there should be cooperation in the development of payments mechanisms along with energetic competition in the area of products. This is so because "[c]ooperation in products blurs distinctions between competing banks, while competition in the area of mechanism generally leads to unproductive fragmentation . . ."[22] It has been argued further that "[w]e must not allow the Payments System to degenerate to a point where consumers have to have checking accounts with several banks in order to pay electronically or where retailers must belong to more than one system in order to serve their customers."[23]

Of course, viewpoints in opposition to coperation and in favor of competition in mechanisms have been formalized. For example, it has been argued that the "nature of the delivery system will in itself define the service parameters" of competing institutions and that a diversity of payments systems "should be allowed to continue so that a true test will come from a competitive evaluation of these alternatives in the marketplace."[24] And of substantial importance is the fact that the pro-competition viewpoint has been strongly supported by the Department of Justice which argues that "law should serve the consumers (large and small) of financial services, and do so by promoting efficiency among competing organizations."[25]

Pragmatically however, it appears that "we are dealing with simultaneous equations, defining product and mechanism, assessing cooperation and competition" subject to the limitation that there exists "no simple rule of thumb for solving such equations since the elements can vary so much."[26]

It should be quite evident that it is indeed a difficult problem to determine exactly where a state of healthy competition degenerates into a state of unhealthy cooperation. And it is equally evident that the ultimate resolution of this problem will have a significant impact on the sponsors of different EFT systems, the convenience of the public at large, and the monitoring and managing of overall economic activity.

Government Participation

For the most part it is agreed that the future electronic payments mechanism should be able to utilize new computer and communication technologies to effect exchanges of value "quickly, reliably and inexpensively" on a scale of extraordinary breadth.[27] Also, the EFT system should have at least the same characteristics of "flexibility, diversity and specialization of functions" as our current payments mechanism.[28]

On this a major issue has been the role of government in achieving the objectives set out for the EFT system. In general, the private sector of the economy favors a minimum of government involvement, one which is preferably restricted to the resolution of legal questions concerning access of competing financial institutions to clearing networks and the protection of individuals' rights in an EFTS economy.[29]

There is a good deal of controversy, however, surrounding a more direct and active government role in the payments mechanism. For example, the direct deposit program of the Treasury is already credited with being a major force for payments system change. But at the same time there exists some fear that any judgments, regarding which financial organizations may participate in the program and on what terms, may well establish precedents capable of doing long-term damage to the competitive position of some institutions while benefiting others.

There is also the danger that the payments mechanism technology required of financial institutions participating in the Treasury program, which is a program of massive scale, may preempt the field of alternative technologies which might otherwise have gained the commitments of competing financial institutions. But it remains to be seen whether such government programs ultimately result in serious anti-competitive "technological preemption," and thereby emasculate the flexibility, diversity, and specialization of functions desired in the EFT system.

Of more immediate concern to the private sector, however, has been the aggressiveness of the Federal Reserve System in establishing a pivotal role for itself in the future EFT economy. More specifically, the Fed has offered these arguments in explanation of why it should assume the ownership and operation of the central components of that system:[30]

1. Monetary policy is indirectly affected by the nation's payments mechanism and the latter should therefore be owned by the Fed which is responsible for such policy.
2. Small financial institutions require the Fed's operation of a public-utility type of electronic payments mechanism in order to survive their competition.
3. The private sector of the economy has been slow to respond to the urgency of implementing a comprehensive electronic payments mechanism.

It should suffice to say that the position of the Federal Reserve has been widely contested and criticized.[31] In the meantime, the exact nature of the government's role in the future EFT system awaits final definition.

Consumer Credit

The expected strong competition among financial organizations to use the new payments technology to enlarge the scope and profitability of their operations has raised the issue of whether EFTS will foster a considerably greater use of consumer credit than now exists.[32] The accumulation of data on individuals in easily-accessed computer files may allow financial organizations to evaluate credit worthiness of potential customers instantaneously, and at minimal cost, leading to more extensive offerings of credit to consumers. Furthermore, it is reasonable to expect that EFTS will promote more widespread lines of credit and overdraft arrangements as financial organizations seek to match their competitors' range of services.[33]

Also it seems reasonable to expect that many individuals, especially the lower income groups, who do not have any systematic relationship with a financial organization, will establish such a relationship if only to be able to participate in a program such as Treasury's direct deposit. Once this customer relationship is established with a financial organization it will probably lead to arrangements for consumer credit as well as to other financial services.[34]

The resolution of the problem of consumer credit in an automated payments mechanism is difficult since it impacts on a wide range of interest groups. In short, the questions to be answered include: How much more credit will be extended with EFTS? What types of consumer credit will be most affected? Who will benefit most from new credit arrangements? How will the cost of credit be affected? What will be the economic impact of more extensive consumer credit arrangements? And finally, what will be the impact on the market shares and economic viability of competing consumer credit grantors?

Freedom of Choice

A problem closely related to that of payments system control is the freedom of choice which will be available to potential participants in an EFTS environment. More specifically, the question arises as to whether the automated payments mechanism is going to enlarge or restrict the range of choices available. Areas of concern to individuals include the choice of financial organizations and services, methods of payment, rates of charge for payments services, and the terms (cash or credit) of payment.[35]

For the merchant the areas of choice cover those of financial organizations with which to deal, the terminal equipment to be purchased or leased, the range of payments services to be offered customers, and the ability to freely substitute one proprietary system for another if the cost-benefit relationships of different systems suggest such substitutions. And participating financial organizations will be concerned about their freedom to choose the individual and commercial customer relationships they will maintain, the suppliers of equipment with whom they will do business, and the time and terms of payment.[36]

The ultimate acceptance and success of EFTS may well depend upon the trade-off between the freedom of choice of potential participants versus the probable benefits to be gained by those very same participants. In any event it is quite likely that any payments system which restricts the range of choices of participants by too great a degree will rapidly fail due to lack of public support.

Individual Privacy

The final unresolved issue to be discussed here is that concerning the potential threat to the privacy of information about individuals posed by EFTS. Along with a progressively larger volume of electronic payments there will be a progressively larger volume of information of all types about individuals readily accessible in computer files. The potential for the abuse of this information by financial or non-financial business organizations, governmental agencies, or other individuals must be recognized and dealt with satisfactorily.[37]

A The range and the detail of the data which will be subject to accumulation and computer filing in an EFTS economy are immense. It is quite possible, for example, that the POS terminals of merchants will not only effect payments for purchases but might also serve to capture data on the individual and his purchases by type of purchase, date of purchase, frequency of purchase, value of purchase, frequency of credit use, credit grantor, and so on. If this same type of information gathering is repeated wherever and whenever the individual must interface with the payments mechanism the accumulation of information on individuals will be overwhelming.

B If such information on individuals is freely shared throughout the business community, individuals might well be subjected to extensive annoying or embarrassing communications. And this fear on the part of consumers is really not allayed by the prospects of government control of computerized information files which might be equally susceptible to misuse for social and political reasons—perhaps menacing participatory democracy itself.

C The all-pervasive concern about individual privacy is an emotional and politically powerful issue concerning the ultimate implementation of electronic funds transfer. Failure to satisfactorily resolve the privacy problem, therefore, could well mean failure to achieve a truly new payments mechanism.

The reader should know, however, that the privacy issue has not been ignored. To the contrary, a considerable amount of study, litigation, and legislation has been addressed to the problem of personal privacy and the remedies for the invasion of privacy.[38]

One of the most prestigious studies on this problem was the July, 1973, report of the Secretary's Advisory Committee on Automated Personal Data Systems. This report, titled "Records, Computers, and the Rights of Citizens," was requested by the Secretary of Health, Education and Welfare in order to "analyze and make recommendations about: Harmful consequences that may result from using automated personal data systems; Safeguards that might protect against potentially harmful consequences; Measures that might afford redress for any harmful consequences; Policy and practice relating to the issuance and use of Social Security numbers."[39]

Following an extensive investigation of the privacy problem the Committee concluded that "the net effect of computerization is that it is becoming much easier for record-keeping systems to affect people than for people to affect record-keeping systems."[40] With this in mind the Committee recommended that a Federal "Code of Fair Information Practice" be enacted which would give legal effect to the following personal data system safeguards:

1. There must be no personal data record-keeping systems whose very existence is secret.
2. There must be a way for an individual to find out what information about him is in a record and how it is used.
3. There must be a way for an individual to prevent information about him that was obtained for one purpose from being used or made available for other purposes without his consent.
4. There must be a way for an individual to correct or amend a record of identifiable information about him.
5. Any organization creating, maintaining, using, or disseminating records of identifiable personal data must assure the reliability of the data for their intended use and must take precautions to prevent misuse of the data.

In conclusion, it can be said that while the privacy problem is indeed difficult there have nevertheless been major efforts to recognize and solve it.[41]

The National Commission on Electronic Fund Transfers

The myriad issues discussed, as well as the economic implications to be considered in the following chapter, prompted Congress to provide for a National Commission on Electronic Fund Transfers: Title II, Public Law 93-495 (H.R. 11221), the Depository Institutions Amendments of 1974, October 28, 1974.

Among other things, it was specified in Sec. 203(a) of Title II that "The Commission shall conduct a thorough study and investigation and recommend appropriate administrative action and legislation necessary in connection with the possible development of public or private electronic fund transfer systems . . ." Specifically, the Commission's study was to take into account at least these elements:

1. The need to preserve competition among financial institutions and other business enterprises using such systems.

2. The need to prevent unfair or discriminatory practices by any financial institution or business enterprise using or desiring to use such systems.
3. The need to afford maximum user and consumer convenience.
4. The need to afford maximum user and consumer rights to privacy and confidentiality.
5. The need to assure that the Government be involved to no greater degree than is necessary.
6. The impact of such systems on economic and monetary policy and on all segments of our society, from large businesses to individual consumers.
7. The implications of such systems on the availability of credit.
8. The implications of such systems expanding internationally and into other forms of electronic communications.
9. The need to protect the legal rights of users and consumers.

The membership of the Commission, according to Sec. 202(a) of Title II, will consist of twenty-six individuals including twelve from agencies of the Federal government, two from state governments, and twelve from the private sector.[42]

CHAPTER 5

ECONOMIC IMPLICATIONS

The changeover to an electronic funds transfer system will have far-reaching economic implications ranging all the way from the near-term expenditures for the hardware and software of such a system to the ultimate reshaping of the traditional theories which currently guide economic policy.

No sector of the American economy will remain unaffected by the new payments mechanism. Government is at the threshold of augmenting significantly its economic power if it should so choose. Financial institutions are moving in the direction of intensified competition as traditional barriers of differentiation erode in the face of new payments technologies. Business and commercial interests stand to benefit from a less costly and more systematic means of making and receiving payments. They will also benefit from instantaneous access to voluminous data at minimal cost along with what that implies for cost control and marketing effectiveness. Finally, consumers should realize greatly increased time and place convenience for an increased range of financial transactions, greater overall credit availability, and earnings on heretofore zero-interest deposit accounts.

Payments System Costs

The most immediate and apparent result of the changeover to EFTS should be that of reducing the approximate $14 billion cost of operating our current payments mechanism. A reduction in the use of cash and currency should result in substantial savings related to the direct production of as well as the cleaning, packaging, distribution, and final destruction of these media of exchange. In addition there will be reduced expenditure on the storage and safe-keeping of cash and currency along with the insurance costs related to such protection of money. Finally, the cost of preventing and insuring against counterfeiting should likewise be reduced.[1]

Of even greater importance should be the exchange system cost savings realized by a dramatic reduction of check use. These savings will encompass direct production, packaging, distribution, check authorization, check verification, forgery, fraud, and float. But the most significant cost savings would appear to be related to the direct substitution of instantaneous electronic transfer for the relatively time consuming and labor intensive check transfer itself.

As stated earlier, however, reliable estimates of the actual cost of operating a comprehensive electronic payments system are not yet available and it must be recognized that the widely discussed dollar savings tend to rely on numerous assumptions. Nevertheless, it is true that a large part of the required infrastructure as well as the technology and know-how for EFTS already exist and are operative. If these initial advantages are not dissipated by the development of an excess number of parallel payments systems, it would appear that the future EFT mechansim will have what amounts to a downward-sloping marginal cost curve rather than the standard upward-sloping curve of the current check-based system.

On a more formal basis, and dollar estimates aside, it has been argued that an increase in the efficiency of the payments mechanism would require but the following:

1. The payment of interest on demand deposit balances;
2. Lower pecuniary and nonpecuniary costs of effecting transactions between financial assets in order to foster optimal portfolio positions and greater sensitivity to market conditions;

3. A lower cost of effecting purchases of goods and services by means of demand accounts; and

4. Consumer bank overdraft facilities which permit consumers to determine their consumption stream with greater flexibility.[2]

In the context of the above criteria, then, it can be said that the EFT systems now operative and the future national system do indeed represent a substantially more efficient payments mechanism for the economy.

Data Capture

The implementation of a national electronic payments network will bring with it the most comprehensive system yet devised for the capture of economic data and other information relating to businesses and individuals. For each and every exchange of value this data may well encompass such items as the consumer's name, address, payment account number, credit rating, place of employment, financial affiliations, products purchased, delivery points of products, terms of purchases, amounts of purchases, days of purchases, and so on. Similar information will also be captured in most inter-business transactions as well as for those between business and government.

The net result of the foregoing will be the accumulation of massive amounts of economic, and in some cases noneconomic, information which will be readily accessible in computer files. On the macro-economic level the utilization of such data will provide almost immediate feedback on the effectiveness of monetary and/or fiscal policies on income, employment, and price levels. It should, therefore, allow much more rapid and appropriate policy adjustments. The accuracy, detail, and quick availability of such information can also be expected to discourage the overall levels of illicit enterprise, tax evasion, and fraud.[3]

On the micro-economic level the accumulation of extensive price, consumption, production, and distribution information could permit a substantial upgrading of the analysis of the economic behavior of, as well as the effectiveness of policies designed for, specific industries or individuals. The flexibility and the reliability of marketing analysis should be subject to considerable improvement while the effectiveness of follow-through advertising could be monitored on a real-time basis, allowing adjustments and corrections to be made in a cybernetic manner.

All of the social and human-engineering sciences should benefit from the wealth of every conceivable type of data being readily available at minimal cost. As a consequence, most hypothetical models of social, psychological, or economic behavior will be no longer afforded the luxury of extended debate or the subsidy of "insufficient data." Rather, they will be proven or disproven almost immediately, resulting in the more efficient allocation of the nation's intellectual resources.

In general, the expansion and dissemination of economic data made possible through EFTS should go a long way toward fulfilling one of the major preconditions of the competitive economic model—that of a state of "perfect knowledge"—and thereby promoting a more perfect market mechanism. The latter result assumes equal knowledge on the part of both buyers and sellers so that market coercion is deterred. However, if buyers, and more specifically consumers, are denied equal access to the relevant market information, or if they are ignorant as to its use, the advent of EFTS could appreciably aggravate already existing market imperfections.

Financial Institutions and Structure

The financial services sector of the economy will be the first and most dramatically affected by EFTS. Commercial banks, savings and loan institutions, mutual savings banks, credit unions, consumer finance companies, and other financial organizations are already being thrust into a rapidly changing and apparently much more competitive economic environment. Furthermore, those changes eventually realized in the financial sector of the economy will have inevitable ramifications for all other economic sectors, especially those which have traditionally maintained an inordinate dependence on a single type of institution for their financing needs.[4] In short, as the financial structure of the economy changes the need for readjustment will be universal rather than insular.

The Hunt Commission. A significant catalyst of the changes currently taking place in the financial sector of the economy was the December, 1971, report of the Hunt Commission, known formally as the President's Commission on Financial Structure and Regulation.

The Hunt Commission was formed in response to the high inflation, volatile interest rates, erratic flows of funds, financial sector illiquidity, and the overall inadequate level of savings which characterized the late 1960s. The mandate of the Commission was to "review and study the structure, operation, and regulation of the private financial institutions in the United States, for the purpose of formulating recommendations that would improve the functioning of the private financial system."[5]

Briefly, the Commission recommended that depository agencies be authorized to offer "a wider range of financial services" and, after a period of transition, "all institutions competing in the same markets do so on an equal basis," in order to serve the public better by: increased competition, more efficient allocation of financial resources, and an expansion of the total savings available for alternative economic needs.[6]

Without waiting for Congress to finalize some form of Financial Institutions Act, the spirit of change of the Hunt Commission and the new technology of electronic payments were brought together by innovative financial institutions which started to prepare themselves for radical change in an EFT economy.

Commercial Banks. In an ironic sense the commercial banking sector of the financial community appears to be facing the greatest relative threat to be posed by the advent of a comprehensive EFT system. This is so in spite of the fact that commercial banks have been in the forefront of the change to an electronic payments mechanism. And it is so irrespective of the fact that the commercial banking system already has in place the most impressive number of EFT clearing and customer interfacing networks.

The threat to the commercial banks comes largely from the rapidly spreading third party payment function for thrift institutions such as savings and loans, mutual savings banks, and credit unions. At the very time the costs of effecting funds transfers are being dramatically reduced, commercial banks stand to lose a significant portion of that funds transfer market to competing financial organizations. And to aggravate the situation, once thrift institutions have their foot in the door they can be expected to challenge commercial banks over a wide range of other services.

Within the commercial banking community itself other types of competitive pressures can be expected. One of these more important competitive developments will be the tendency for geographic barriers to become progressively less meaningful in the marketing of bank services.[7] The technology of EFTS will permit any commercial bank, or other financial institution for that matter, to enter any market area regardless of location.

Pressures are building even now to provide for both universal statewide branching and ultimately nationwide branching. And since the computer and communications technology of EFTS literally does away with the distance-related costs of banking there no longer exists an economic restraint on the desire for branching. Furthermore, liberal branching is viewed as one way commercial banks might offset a loss of market share to their thrift competitors.

One example of the impact of EFT technology on branch banking was the December, 1974, ruling of the Comptroller of the Currency which approved the installation of off-premises customer bank communications terminals (CBCTs) for national banks.

This ruling permits national banks to establish, without geographic restrictions, electronic terminals through which an existing bank customer can initiate transactions resulting in a cash withdrawal from his account, a transfer between his checking and savings accounts, and payment transfers from his account into accounts maintained by other bank customers.[8] The ruling also provides that these terminals may be unmanned and operated by the customer himself at any convenient location the bank chooses, such as a shopping center; they may also be located on the premises of a business establishment, such as a supermarket, and may be manned by any employee of the establishment. In a statement accompanying the ruling, the Comptroller said that these terminals are "the forerunner of an expected family of customer operated electronic terminals which will change the face of the banking industry."[9]

Traditional banking practices can be expected to change somewhat in still another way: The competition for, and the costs of retaining customer deposits in, an EFT economy will increase. For example, the Hunt Commission recommended the eventual phasing out of Regulation Q which governs the rate ceiling differentials applied to savings deposits in commercial banks as opposed to thrift institutions.[10] In addition, a number of financial institutions have undertaken to offer what amount to interest-paying checking accounts (as discussed in Chapter 2). The net result will be an overall greater competition for customer deposits and a higher cost for retaining those deposits. This could well lead to a situation in which commercial banks place less emphasis on deposit-based revenues and considerably more emphasis on service- and transactions-based revenues.

In summary then, it would appear that the future EFTS environment will lead to a significant role for thrift institutions in third party transfers—at the expense of commercial banks. Also, the traditional geographic barriers to competition will eventually yield to EFT-based statewide and nationwide branch banking, with a consequent depletion in the number of smaller commercial banks which are unable to compete. The larger banks and bank holding companies can be expected to compete vigorously by the introduction of as many proprietary EFT services, terminal installations, and other differentiating products as possible. And finally, a change in emphasis from deposit-based to transactions-based revenues appears likely as the overall cost of attracting and retaining customer deposits increases.

Thrift Institutions. For the moment at least, it appears that the major beneficiaries of the developing EFTS will be thrift institutions such as savings and loans, and mutual savings banks. Not only will these institutions realize all of the operational cost savings associated with electronic payments technology but they will very probably assume a major role in a market heretofore closed to them—third party payments.

The great success of the NOW account programs in Massachusetts and New Hampshire, the Transmatic Money System in Nebraska, the payment order accounts in New York, and so on, have all proven the high inclination of the public to utilize the thrift industry, and thereby interest bearing accounts, for the purpose of third party payments.

Also of apparent advantage to the thrift sector of the financial community is the movement to increase the range of financial services which can be offered by both savings and loan associations and mutual savings banks. For example, the Hunt Commission recommended that thrifts be allowed to expand their deposit services for consumers and also that they be permitted more investment and lending activities.[11] On a practical level, this means that thrifts will become progressively a more important factor in checking accounts, consumer loans, credit cards, and other family financial services.

It would appear that thrift institutions are going to benefit substantially from the assumption of a new third party payment service heretofore denied them. Along with this new service the thrift industry can be expected to expand into numerous other areas of financial services previously associated with the commercial banking system or other financial organizations. Finally, the thrift industry, which in recent years has shown itself to be both very astute and very aggressive, can be expected to promote a greater number of sophisticated national clearing networks such as MINTS in order to increase its competitive stature and, even more importantly, its financial autonomy.

Other Financial Organizations. The most commonly known depository institutions, and the ones most likely to experience the most radical changes through EFTS, are the commercial banks, savings and loans, and the mutual savings banks, all of which will be engaged in vigorous competition for consumers' deposits. This does not mean, however, that other financial intermediaries will not be impacted by EFTS.

It has already been seen, for example, that credit unions, which are large in number and which have been rapidly increasing their share of the consumer credit market, have followed the lead of the savings and loan associations and the mutual savings banks in an effort to establish both third party payment services and nationwide clearing networks.

The problem facing the credit union industry, however, is that a large percentage of their institutions are relatively small and lack operational and product sophistication. For the latter, therefore, the EFTS phenomenon represents a substantial threat to their survival. They simply will not be able to compete against the convenience and scope of services offered by their competitors and a large number can be expected to fail.

But the larger and more sophisticated credit unions should be able to exploit EFT technology in order to make themselves formidable competitors in the financial services market. These institutions already have minimal overhead expenses and EFTS should allow them to minimize their current labor costs even as they increase their scope of services.

On balance, credit unions should benefit from the cost savings of the new electronic payments technology while they simultaneously make use of the reservoir of goodwill of their members to assume a growing role in third party payments, consumer loans, and a host of other financial services.

Consumer finance companies are for the most part nondepository in nature and completely specialized in the extension of consumer credit. Their operating expenses are dominated by labor costs and the cost of borrowed funds while their revenues are dominated by finance charges earned on loans made.

The advent of EFTS can be expected to impact negatively on both the number and the market share of consumer finance companies. This will be due to the sharp increase in competition coming from commercial banks and thrift institutions which will introduce and vigorously promote pre-established lines of credit to be activated at the point of sale by their deposit account holders. As a result, the latter institutions will tend to preempt a certain portion of what has traditionally been the consumer finance company market. In essence, consumer finance companies as presently structured, that is, being nondepository, will be unable to enter the third party payments market while at the same time depository financial organizations will enter the consumer credit market in force.

At the same time, however, EFT technology will provide the wherewithal for substantial labor cost savings as well as the real-time access to that customer data required for superior credit-granting decisions and the monitoring of accounts. In both of these respects, therefore, consumer finance companies can expect to benefit from EFTS. In fact, the well-managed consumer finance company which is successful at protecting its share of the market, while exploiting the cost-saving characteristics of EFTS, should be a more profitable enterprise in the future than it has been traditionally.

Specialization. It has already been seen that the advent of EFTS will provide a vehicle whereby a large number of specialized institutions can increase the scope of their financial services. The most obvious example is once again the movement of thrift institutions into traditional commercial banking areas. However, the expected competition among financial organizations will surely extend far beyond that of just third party payments as each group of institutions attempts to match the services of competitors. The net result should be one of many more financial services offered by many more financial organizations at lower overall prices, and ultimately a decrease in the differentiation between such financial organizations.

Regulation. The outlook for the regulation of financial institutions is also one of change to be accelerated by EFTS. For example, Congress continues to consider a Financial Institutions Act, based on the report of the Hunt Commission, which calls for a comprehensive restructuring of the financial community with an eye towards increasing interinstitutional competition and eliminating those regulations which impede such competition. In general, it appears that Regulation Q will be phased out and replaced by competitively established interest payments on deposits; that commercial banks will be allowed statewide branchbanking; and that the thrift industry will be granted full permission for third party payments and other financial services.

Nonfinancial Sectors

The coming electronic payments mechanism will have an appreciable impact on the operations of practically all of the nonfinancial sectors of the economy. And in almost every case this impact will be beneficial as business organizations and individuals learn to utilize EFTS to their advantage and as financial institutions compete to attract and hold customers through low-cost and comprehensive EFTS programs.

Retailers. The retail sector of the economy perhaps stands to gain most relatively speaking from EFTS. Automated payments, credit authorization, inventory control, marketing analysis, will add up to a significant new capacity to control costs, adjust rapidly to changing market conditions, establish advantageous POS service arrangements, and, most importantly, improve their profit position.

It is almost universally accepted that the long-term success of EFTS will largely depend upon its effectiveness in terms of point-of-sale applications. And quite obviously the retail establishment in most cases is the point of sale. For this reason the retail sector of the economy can be expected to possess a great deal of leverage on the ultimate structuring of EFTS.

Large retail chains already have extensive internal point-of-sale systems which are cost justified by their own economies of scale. It is unlikely, therefore, that financial intermediaries of whatever type will be able to capture much, if any, of the business of these large chains without accepting conditions very favorable to the latter.

The case of small retail establishments will probably be of the opposite nature. For these smaller establishments financial intermediaries can be expected to market a "payments package" tailored to the needs of the retail client in terms of hardware, software, customer access device, consumer credit control, and electronic accounting services. But here too, the profit objectives of financial intermediaries in supplying EFT services are likely to be compromised because of the large number of competing payments systems from which the retailer can choose.

More specifically, EFTS will lead to the widespread installation of POS terminals in retail establishments. These terminals, perhaps very sophisticated electronic cash registers (ECRs), will be used to authorize payments, verify accounts, extend credit, provide for cash deposits or withdrawals. The particular transaction capabilities of a given terminal will be negotiable between the retailer and the system supplier and it can be expected that the retailer will be in a good position to exact favorable terms.

Large retailers will develop, install, and operate their own EFT systems and issue their own customer card for accessing purposes. In addition, these large retail organizations can be expected to enter the competition among financial institutions and others for the installing and operating of EFT packages for other business organizations.

In terms of their own operations most retail users of EFT systems can expect to realize at least the following economic benefits:

1. An appreciable decrease in the amount of time required to effect retail transactions.
2. The improvement of control over the amount of loss associated with credit and fraudulent transactions.
3. A decrease in the cost of account collections as preauthorized debit arrangements are expanded.
4. Improved cash management as smaller balances are required to be on hand for check-cashing purposes.
5. A substantial decline in personnel expense as progressively more of the retail operation, from bookkeeping to check-out, becomes automated.
6. Improved inventory control as computerized checkstands monitor surpluses and scarcities on a real-time basis.
7. Substantially improved marketing based on extensive data capture at the point of sale.

The food-retailing industry, as a case in point, is already well along in the design and use of computer and communications technology for the very reasons cited above. The emphasis here has been on the development of internal systems centered around ECRs and the industry-designed Universal Product Code (UPC).

The success of the ECR/UPC systems has been evidenced by the fact that there were only a handful of such installations in the early 1970s whereas it has been estimated that "some 300 stores will be installed by 1975 year end."[12] Furthermore, the food chain industry anticipates that by the late 1970s automated installations will provide "a return on . . . investment of 35%."[13]

Other Business. Non-retail business organizations can also expect to benefit substantially from the implementation of EFTS. Cash management will be improved as business organizations synchronize the automated receiving and making of payments and hold but a minimum of non-interest earning deposit balances.

For a large number of businesses the preauthorized crediting of employee payrolls will eliminate the time consuming and costly preparation of individual checks while at the same time the problems of fraud, forgery, and burdensome record keeping will be reduced. Conversely, in those situations where preauthorized debits, or receipts of payment, can be arranged the business organization will benefit from a reduction in the costs of collections, late payments, safeguarding of receipts, and so on.

In general, business organizations will benefit from the improvement in data collection in all areas of their operation. This should ultimately manifest itself in an improvement of marketing, distribution, production, and investment decisions.

Finally, since there will be intense competition among financial institutions seeking to attract and hold customers, business organizations should be able to contract for complete financial service packages which will save them time as well as the considerable expenditure on the in-house operation which would have otherwise been needed.

Government. The government sector at all levels ought to benefit from the decreased costs of both making and receiving payments. Direct deposit programs for recurring benefits and payrolls will save time, handling, distribution, loss, forgery, and fraud expenses. Extensive information on all economic sectors will provide for greater control over illicit activities, reduced expenditure on regulatory enforcement, and a substantial decrease in tax revenue losses. Finally, comprehensive real-time information on both macro-economic and micro-economic processes should contribute to a significant improvement in monetary and fiscal policies and thereby promote more stable economic growth.

Consumers. On balance, the prospect is that for consumers the advent of EFTS will be beneficial. The cost savings realized throughout the economy will be shared, in one form or another, with consumers. And the widespread adoption of interest-bearing demand deposit accounts, known as the "single account," will also be to the advantage of the consumer.

Consumers will also have the opportunity to select from a wider range of financial services being offered by a larger number of competing financial institutions. One result of this will be greater time and place convenience for consumer financial transactions. Another result will be the greater availability of consumer credit, especially in the form of preauthorized lines which can be activated at the point of sale. At the same time the occurrences of defaults, personal bankruptcies, and other credit difficulties should be decreased because of the abundance of credit-rating data which will be readily available to credit granting institutions.

In spite of the above advantages, however, there remain some areas of concern to consumers. The most obvious disadvantage, for example, involves the loss of "float," that is, the time which elapses between contracting to pay and actually making payment. In addition, some consumers, in spite of better overall controls, may have difficulty in managing their use of readily available and conveniently accessed lines of credit. There is also the potential problem of errors in billing which may prove difficult to correct, especially if consumers lose the "stop payment" option they now have with checks and credit cards. Finally, there are the problems of card theft, the feeling of loss of personal identity, and the general negative reaction to progressively more computerization of lifestyle.

Economic Theory and Policy

Certainly, EFTS will have a significant impact on economic theory and policy. Perhaps the area which will be most affected is monetary theory. For example, the advent of the single account, which is an interest-earning demand deposit, will probably require the redefining of the traditional M_1 money stock measure. Also, the formulation of monetary policy will have to take into account the fact that EFTS will enable a smaller monetary base to support a given level of economic activity due to an increase in velocity. This implies, in addition, that the overall level of savings in the economy should be relatively greater with EFTS than without.

It will probably be necessary to discard, or substantially modify, those models of financial market behavior which have been developed through years of experience with well defined financial intermediaries and a fixed institutional environment. EFTS is the cutting edge of radical structural and regulatory changes now taking place in the financial sector of the economy. Therefore, monetary theory and policy which does not recognize and quickly adapt to this new reality will prove itself more harmful than not.

Another area of major economic concern has to do with the ultimate role of the government, or more specifically the Federal

Reserve, in the automated exchange mechanism of the future. Surely, the greater the number of private and competing payments networks which are allowed the lesser will be the government's economic power. If, on the other hand, only one universal clearing system is condoned the potential power and control of the government over all aspects of business and individual economic activity will be enhanced immensely.

The data-capturing capacity of an EFT system should allow economists to quickly formulate and/or adjust monetary and fiscal policies to the exigencies at hand. It should also go a long way toward providing the type of detailed and continuous data required for the thorough construction and evaluation of alternative economic models. The specialized area of econometrics will probably exploit EFT systems for what would amount to an "on-line" and cybernetic estimation and re-estimation of the parameters of econometric models.

The Major Implications

The abundance of material included in the preceding discussions should not be allowed to obscure the major economic implications of an electronic funds transfer system.[14] First, an electronic payments mechanism universally recognizes and respects the time value of money: credit is charged for when given; debits and credits are made when due; float is minimized or eliminated. Second, EFTS substantially reduces the direct and indirect costs of transactions: electronic impulses replace paper; time and place convenience is maximized; prenegotiated credit lines are common; information flows reduce costly market imperfections. Third, the EFT system is a single account system: zero-interest demand deposits are phased out; financial institutions are less differentiated and more competitive; the money supply requires redefinition; the theory of financial markets must be reshaped. And finally, an EFT system is an information and communications system: massive amounts of data are captured and made available at minimal cost; individual, business, and government decision-making is improved; consumer credit problems are better controlled; geographic barriers to market entry disappear.

CHAPTER 6

SUMMARY AND CONCLUSIONS

The dismantling of one outmoded exchange mechanism in favor of another, more advanced, mechanism has occurred periodically throughout the history of economic society. Simple barter, modified barter, metallic money, fractional reserves, and our current coin, currency, and check-based system were all the by-products of the dynamics of economic evolution. And each successive exchange mechanism was itself associated with an alteration in the balance of economic power within society.

The movement toward an electronic payments mechanism is now well under way and appears to be irreversible. It is the result of the convergence of such forces as the already high and rising costs of an exchange mechanism based on paper transfers, the ready availability of the required technology, and the combined pressures for change on the part of both public and private institutions.

Current payments system costs have been estimated to be in the neighborhood of $14 billion, the bulk of which are attributable to the time and handling costs of checks. In addition to the latter, the current payments mechanism is encumbered by the costs of producing, recording, distributing, and safeguarding the major coin, currency, and check media of exchange. All of the foregoing costs stand to be substantially reduced in an electronic funds transfer environment.

Precursors of the EFT system of the future have been evident for some time in such clearing networks as the Federal Reserve Wire, the Bank Wire, and the European-style GIRO systems. More recently the Federal Reserve has augmented the capacity of its own clearing network by means of Regional Check Processing Centers while the major bank card systems have been rapidly upgrading their own independent and parallel clearing networks.

Strong and persistent pressures for new payments arrangements have been forthcoming from practically all financial intermediaries as well as the government sector of the economy. Commercial banks have been actively promoting electronic payments systems in order to decrease the relatively high cost of paper transactions in the current exchange mechanism. Thrift institutions have been in the forefront of the drive for fundamental structural changes in the financial community: In brief, thrift institutions hope to exploit the cutting edge of new payments technology to augment their scope of operations by offering third party transfers, consumer loans, and a wide range of other financial services.

The government sector of the economy has been deeply involved in both designing and exerting pressures for significant innovations in the exchange mechanism. The objectives in this case have been those of sharply reducing the costs of printing and distributing federal agency check disbursements as well as to reduce the losses of fraud and theft associated with such disbursements. The Department of the Treasury, the Social Security Administration, the Department of the Air Force, and the Federal Reserve System have all been involved in the promotion of direct deposit programs for federal payrolls and federal recurring benefits. Similar programs are expected to spread rapidly throughout most major federal agencies as EFTS expertise, experience, and capacity is built up.

Other federal agencies such as the Federal Reserve Board, the Federal Home Loan Bank Board, the Federal Deposit Insurance Corporation, the Comptroller of the Currency, and the Department of Justice are also taking initiatives in the promotion of automated payments experiments, the evaluation of experiment results, and the drafting of recommendations on the optimum structure of the future electronic payments system.

In a very narrow sense EFTS can be thought of as nothing other than an extension of our current payments mechanism in which paper is replaced by electronic impulse. To most observers and potential participants, however, EFTS has come to embrace a wide range of new service and convenience arrangements which render it a revolutionary rather than an evolutionary development in exchange mechanisms.

Most of the basic elements of the prospective electronic funds transfer system can be classified as having: (1) clearing network characteristics; (2) remote service or point-of-sale characteristics; and (3) preauthorized debit/credit characteristics.

The automated clearing house is the focal point of the new payments mechanism since it is regionally based and serves both local clearing requirements as well as the ultimate interconnect needs to both national clearing networks and local point-of-sale systems.

The economies of scale required to make EFTS a truly cost-effective exchange mechanism will be realized only when public participation or interfacing is achieved through the widespread installation and utilization of POS terminals. Some form of plastic coded card appears to be the major vehicle for individual access to the automated payments mechanism.

A wide range of problems associated with the transition to electronic funds transfer remain unresolved. For example, payments system control as manifested in standards, ownership, accessibility, and regulation has yet to be determined. Likewise, the allocation of costs among payments system participants remains an open issue. And the problem of establishing an acceptable dividing line between cooperation and competition in the development and implementation of EFT systems is complicated by anti-trust considerations.

Along with solutions to these problems, resolutions must also be found on the degree and form of government participation in an EFTS environment as well as on the desirability of relatively more consumer credit, the freedom of choice of all sectors of the economy, and the very critical implications of EFTS for individual privacy.

Certainly, it must be recognized that as of yet there are multiple payments systems, and some form of "shake-out" can be expected in the not-too-distant future. However, a public utility type of monopoly payments mechanism has not yet received a great deal of support and is probably an unlikely resolution of EFTS problems in the foreseeable future.

In terms of probable economic impact, EFTS can be expected to be relatively more beneficial to thrift institutions in the financial sector of the economy and to retailers in the nonfinancial sector of the economy. In general, less specialization and less regulation will characterize the financial community with EFTS than is now the case.

In summary, an EFTS economy is one in which the time value of money is recognized, lower direct and indirect costs of transactions are realized, zero-interest accounts are phased out in favor of single accounts, and massive information flows improve decision making and contribute to more competitive markets.

Finally, the National Commission on Electronic Fund Transfers has been empowered to thoroughly investigate all of the ramifications of EFT and to recommend within two years appropriate administrative and legislative action on public and private EFT systems. It may well be, however, that the dynamics of our current economic society will have gone a long way during this time toward defining the ultimate structure of an automated payments mechanism on its own, thus relegating the Commission's work and recommendations to a relatively superfluous status.

GLOSSARY OF ACRONYMS

The following is a list of common EFTS acronyms

ACH	Automated Clearing House
APD	Automated Payment and Deposit
ATM	Automated Teller Machine
BASE	BankAmericard Service Exchange
CACHA	California Automated Clearing House Association
CBCT	Customer Bank Communications Terminal
CDM	Cash Dispensing Machine
COPE	Committee on Paperless Entries (of Atlanta)
DDA	Demand Deposit Account
DDD	Direct Deposit of Dividends
DDP	Direct Deposit of Payroll
ECR	Electronic Cash Register
EDP	Electronic Data Processing
EFT	Electronic Funds Transfer
EFTS	Electronic Funds Transfer System(s)
EMTS	Electronic Money Transfer System
EPS	Electronic Payments System
GACHA	Georgia Automated Clearing House Association
GIRO	European-Style Credit-Based Payments System
INAS	Interbank National Authorization System
ISO	International Standards Organization
MAPS	Monetary and Payment Systems Planning Committee

GLOSSARY OF ACRONYMS

MICR	Magnetic Ink Character Recognition
MINTS	Mutual Institutions National Transfer System, Inc.
NACHA	National Automated Clearing House Association
NEACH	New England Automated Clearing House Association
NETS	Nebraska Electronic Transfer System
NOW	Negotiable Order of Withdrawal
PAL	Preapproved Loan
PAP	Prearranged Payments
PAT	Prearranged Transfers
PEP	Paperless Electronic Payments
PIN	Personal Identification Number
POS	Point-of-Sale
POW	Pay Order of Withdrawal
RCPC	Regional Check Processing Center
RSU	Remote Service Unit
SCOPE	Special Committee on Paperless Entries (of California)
SPC	Switching and Processing Center
SWIFT	Society for Worldwide Interbank Financial Telecommunication
TMS	Transmatic Money System
UPC	Universal Product Code
WOW	Western Order of Withdrawal

NOTES

Chapter 1

1. For a thorough history of money and exchange mechanisms see Mueller, Frederick W., *Money and Banking*, 1st ed., McGraw-Hill, Inc., 1959, Chapters 1-9.

Chapter 2

1. Arthur D. Little, Inc., *The Consequences of Electronic Funds Transfer: A Technology Assessment of Movement Towards A Less Cash/Less Check Society*, Vol. 1, National Science Foundation, January 30, 1975, p. 98.
2. Arthur D. Little, Inc., *An Assessment of Less Cash/Less Check Technology*, National Science Foundation, 1974, p. 9.
3. American Bankers Association, *Executive Report of the Monetary and Payments System Planning Committee*, Washington, D.C., 1971.
4. Ibid.
5. McConnell, Richard M. M., "The Payments System: How it Works Now and Why it is Changing," *Banking*, May, 1974, p. 35.
6. Ibid.
7. Federal Reserve Board of Governors, *The Federal Reserve System: Purposes and Functions*, Board of Governors, Washington, D.C., 1974, p. 22.
8. Mitchell, George W., "Role of the Federal Reserve in the Payments Mechanism," speech at the First Annual Payments System Policy Conference, Chicago, Illinois, December 2, 1974.
9. McConnell, p. 35.

10. Ibid.
11. Federal Reserve Board of Governors, pp. 20-21.
12. Mitchell, p. 7.
13. Flannery, Mark J. and Dwight M. Jaffee, *The Economic Implications of an Electronic Monetary Transfer System,* D. C. Heath and Company, Lexington, Massachusetts, 1973, pp. 45-46. Also Waage, Thomas O., "GIRO Credit-Transfer Plan Could be EFTS Alternative," *American Banker,* October 29, 1973.
14. Mathis, Marilyn, "How Third-Party-Payment Devices are Spreading Across the U.S.," *Banking,* June, 1973, p. 78.
15. McConnell, Richard M. M., "What NOW Account Battle is All About," *Banking,* June, 1973, p. 29.
16. Ibid., p. 30.
17. Furash, Edward E., "Competitive Pressures: The NOW as a Case Study," speech at the First Annual Payments System Policy Conference, Chicago, Illinois, December 2, 1974. Also see Gibson, Katharine, "The Early History and Initial Impact of NOW Accounts," *New England Economic Review,* January-February, 1975, pp. 17-26.
18. McConnell, pp. 29-31, pp. 92-93.
19. Mathis, Marilyn, "How (and Where) Thrifts are Making Gains in Providing Third-Party Payment Services," *Banking,* December, 1974, p. 36.
20. Ibid., p. 32.
21. Ibid., p. 38.
22. Ibid., p. 38.
23. *Credit Union Magazine,* November, 1974, pp. 6-7.
24. *Bank Marketing,* June, 1974, pp. 7-8.
25. Ibid.
26. Nebraska Bankers Association, *Nebraska Electronic Transfer System,* 1974.
27. Richman, Alan, "MINTS: Sweet Taste of EFTS for Hungry Savings Banks," *Bank Systems & Equipment,* February, 1974.
28. Brooke, Phillip, "MINTS Has Specs on New Debit Card," *American Banker,* January 23, 1975, pp. 1, 14.
29. Ibid., p. 14.
30. *FHLBB Journal,* "Board Proposes Amendments to EFTS Regulations," June, 1974, p. 28.
31. Ibid.
32. Brooke, Phillip, "FHLBB Pushes EFTS Expansion for S&Ls," *American Banker,* August 5, 1974, pp. 1, 14.
33. Department of the Treasury, *Direct Deposit of Federal Recurring Benefits,* January, 1975.
34. Ibid., Part I, p. 1.
35. Ibid., pp. 2-3.
36. Ibid., pp. 3-4.
37. Ibid., p. 4.
38. Department of the Treasury, *Direct Deposit—Electronic Funds Transfer Program for Federal Recurring Benefit Payments,*

September, 1974, p. 7.
39. *Thruput,* No. 3, American Bankers Association, Washington, December, 1974.
40. Ibid.
41. *NACHA Quarterly Update,* National Automated Clearing House Association, Washington, October, 1974, p. 1.

Chapter 3

1. Skoba, Roy A., "The Impact of Marketing on Electronic Funds Transfers," *United States Investor/Eastern Banker,* September 23, 1974, pp. 17-18.
2. Poppen, Jon C., "New Marketing Opportunities and Potential for Profit," speech at First Annual Payments System Policy Conference, Chicago, Illinois, December 2, 1974.
3. Sprague, Richard E., "Electronic Funds Transfer Systems: The Status in Mid-1974," Part I, *Computers and People,* August, 1974, p. 34.
4. Ibid., p. 35.
5. *Federal Reserve Bulletin,* December, 1973, pp. 875-876. Also see Adams, William M., "Time to Automate the Clearing House?" *Banking,* May, 1973, pp. 74, 118-119.
6. Federal Reserve Board of Governors, *The Purposes and Functions of the Federal Reserve System,* Washington, D.C., September, 1974.
7. Homrighausen, Paul E., "One Large Step Toward Less-Check: The California Automated Clearing House System," *The Business Lawyer,* July, 1973, p. 1143.
8. Ibid.
9. Campbell, R. R., "New England's Automated Clearing House," *FHLBB Journal,* July, 1974, pp. 20-21.
10. Homrighausen, p. 1143.
11. *NACHA Quarterly Update,* National Automated Clearing House Association, Washington, D.C., October, 1974, p. 3.
12. Thompson, Robert O., "Payment Systems in 1980," *FHLBB Journal,* January, 1974, p. 37.
13. Hall, William, "SWIFT: The Revolution Round the Corner," *The Banker,* June, 1973 and Brooke, Phillip, "SWIFT, Worldwide Payments Network, Enters Active Phase Today in Brussels," *American Banker,* May 3, 1973.
14. Fisher, John F., "Remote Banking: Point of Sale and Automated Teller Services," speech at the First Annual Payments System Policy Conference, Chicago, Illinois, December 2, 1974.
15. *United States Investor/Eastern Banker,* January 13, 1975, p. 27.
16. Skoba, p. 17.
17. Fisher.
18. O'Neal, Milton, "Point of Sale Systems: 'Still Testing,'" *Banking,* January, 1974, pp. 21-23, 88-89. Also Asher, Joe, "What the

Point-of-Sale Revolution Means to Banks," *Banking*, August, 1974, pp. 32-34, 77-79.

19. Knight, Robert E., "The Changing Payments Mechanisms: Electronic Funds Transfer Arrangements," *Monthly Review*, Federal Reserve Bank of Kansas City, July-August, 1974, pp. 15-16.
20. Ibid., p. 16.
21. Ibid.
22. *Payment Systems Newsletter*, Vol. 5, No. 11, November, 1973, p. 1.
23. *Payment Systems Newsletter*, Vol. 6, No. 7, July, 1974, p. 2.
24. Ibid.
25. *Payment Systems Newsletter*, Vol. 6, No. 12, December, 1974, p. 1.
26. Ibid., pp. 3-4.
27. Anderson, Douglas D., "EFTS: State of the Art," *United States Investor/Eastern Banker*, September 9, 1974, pp. 27-29.
28. Knight, pp. 13-14.
29. Ibid., p. 14.
30. Ibid., pp. 14-15. Also Anderson, pp. 27-29.
31. *NACHA Quarterly Update*, National Automated Clearing House Association, Washington, D.C., October, 1974, p. 6.
32. Adams, Kenneth M., "The Bank Card: Yesterday, Today, Tomorrow," *Banking*, September, 1974, pp. 118-120; Reistad, Dale L., "EFTS Technology Spawns New Payments Products," *Savings & Loan News*, October, 1973, pp. 90-91; Elfrank, Charles A., "New 'Jobs' Ahead for Bank Cards," *Banking*, September, 1973, p. 115; "No Passbook Savings: Not a Question of Whether, Only of How Soon," *Savings & Loan News*, November, 1973, pp. 54-59; "Pick a Card, Any Card," *Savings & Loan News*, October, 1974, pp. 46-51.
33. *Payment Systems Newsletter*, Vol. 6, No. 2, February, 1974, p. 6.
34. "Credit-Card and Check-Credit Plans at Commercial Banks," *Federal Reserve Bulletin*, Board of Governors, Washington, D.C., September, 1973.
35. Hock, Dee W., "Role of the Bank Card," speech at First Annual Payments System Policy Conference, Chicago, Illinois, December 2, 1974.
36. Flannery, Mark J. and Dwight M. Jaffee, *The Economic Implications of an Electronic Monetary Transfer System*, D. C. Heath and Company, Lexington, Massachusetts, 1973, pp. 51-55.
37. Ibid.
38. "National BankAmericard Begins Nationwide Electronic Interchange," National BankAmericard, Inc., San Francisco, California, November 1, 1974. Also *Payment Systems Newsletter*, Vol. 6, No. 11, November, 1974, p. 4.

Chapter 4

1. Baker, Donald I., "Competition, Monopoly and Electronic Banking," *Consumer Credit 1975*, Practising Law Institute, New York, 1975, p. 378.

2. Duffy, Helene, "Major Policy Issues Affect Prospects for EFTS," *American Banker*, September 16, 1974, p. 18.

3. 38 Fed. Reg. 32953 (Nov. 29, 1973).

4. Mitchell, George W., *Federal Reserve Bulletin*, Washington, D.C., December, 1973, p. 878.

5. Ibid., pp. 877-878. Also see *Payment Systems Newsletter*, Vol. 5, No. 11, November, 1973, p. 4.

6. Arthur D. Little, Inc., *An Assessment of Less Cash/Less Check Technology*, National Science Foundation, February, 1974, pp. 46-51.

7. *Payment Systems Newsletter*, Vol. 6, No. 4, April, 1974, p. 6.

8. "ABA Announces Study to Develop EFTS Model for Members, State Associations," *American Banker*, January 8, 1975, p. 1. Also "ABA Steps Up Efforts to Aid Localities in EFTS Planning," *Banking*, January, 1975, pp. 40, 89.

9. Arthur D. Little, Inc., pp. 46-51.

10. See, for example, "Justice Department Requests Information from S F Fed on Why CACHA Is Not Allowing Direct Access to S&Ls," *Payment Systems Newsletter*, Vol. 7, No. 1, January, 1975, p. 1 and Brooke, Phillip, "Thrifts Given Direct Access to NY ACH, SBANYS Says; Action Is a Breakthrough," *American Banker*, January 27, 1975, pp. 1, 14.

11. *Payment Systems Newsletter*, Vol. 6, No. 9, September, 1974, p. 5.

12. "Credit Unions Buy a Kansas Bank," *Business Week*, November 30, 1974, p. 53.

13. *Payment Systems Newsletter*, Vol. 6, No. 5, May, 1974, p. 1. For the most part, however, the posture of the commercial banking sector of the economy relative to the ownership issue has been one of strong support for the continued existence of privately owned and competitive EFT systems. See, for example, "Electronic Funds Transfer Systems: One, Two or More? Bank-Run or Fed-Run?, *Banking*, July, 1974, pp. 26-27, 52-54, 62-63. Also Brooke, Phillip, "ABA Asks Reg. J Provide for Both Fed and Private Payments Mechanisms," *American Banker*, March 18, 1974, pp. 1, 8.

14. Baker, p. 379. And Baker also argues that regulation and regulatory agencies have been anti-competitive. See, for example, "Maybe It's Time to Make Changes in the System," *The Bankers Magazine*, Vol. 157, No. 4, Autumn, 1974, pp. 70-71.

15. This is made quite evident by doing no more than scanning headlines such as the following: "FHLBB Pushes EFTS Expansion for S&Ls," *American Banker*, August 5, 1974, p. 1; "FHLBB Approves 13 Applications by S&Ls for Remote EFT Units, 1

Denied, 30 Pending," *American Banker*, February 7, 1975, p. 1; "FHLBB Asks Consumer Lending, Checks at S&Ls," *American Banker*, February 7, 1975, p. 1; Comptroller of the Currency "Smith Issues Ruling Granting Electronic Terminals Without Geographic Limitation," *American Banker*, December 13, 1974, p. 1; "Mo. Commissioner Sues to Block CBCTs of FNB St. Louis Under Antibranch Law." *American Banker*, January 7, 1975, p. 1; "Conn. Atty. Gen. Says Paying Bills by Phone is Illegal Now," *American Banker*, January 22, 1975, p. 1; "Conference of State Bank Supervisors Warns of Fed Involvement in EFTS," *Payment Systems Newsletter*, Vol. 6, No. 4, April, 1974, p. 1; "Legalities Stall Washington's Joint EFTS," *American Banker*, September 4, 1974, p. 1.

16. Arthur D. Little, Inc., "Summary Report on Proceedings of a Conference on Technology Assessment of the Less-Cash/Less-Check Society," Washington, D.C., June 13, 1974, p. 3.

17. Ibid.

18. Brandel, Roland E. and Zane O. Gresham, "Electronic Payments: Government Intervention or New Frontier for Private Initiative," *The Business Lawyer*, Vol. 29, July, 1974, p. 1144.

19. Welman, Jr., J. C., "Timing for Change: Cooperative Development in EFTS," speech at First Annual Payments System Policy Conference, Chicago, Illinois, December 3, 1974.

20. Ibid.

21. Brooke, Phillip, "Electronic Funds Transfer Systems," *American Banker Reprint Service*, No. 165, p. 6.

22. Sullivan, Barry F., "An Issues Overview of the Present and Future Payments Systems," speech at First Annual Payments System Policy Conference, Chicago, Illinois, December 2, 1974.

23. Welman, Jr.

24. Glasser, Paul F., "EFTS Competitive Developments," speech at First Annual Payments System Policy Conference, Chicago, Illinois, December 3, 1974.

25. Baker, Donald I., "Competition, Monopoly and Electronic Banking," p. 380. Mr. Baker is Deputy Assistant Attorney General, Antitrust Division, Department of Justice.

26. Sullivan.

27. Brandel and Gresham, pp. 1134-1136.

28. Ibid.

29. Arthur D. Little, Inc., "Summary Report on Proceedings of a Conference on Technology Assessment of the Less-Cash/Less-Check Society," Washington, D.C., June 13, 1974, p. 6.

30. Brandel and Gresham, p. 1137.

31. See, for example: Brandel and Gresham, pp. 1137-1146; Baker, pp. 388-400; Brooke, Phillip, "ABA Asks Reg. J Provide for Both Fed and Private Payments Mechanisms," *American Banker*, March 18, 1974, pp. 1, 8; "Conference of State Bank Supervisors Warns of Fed Involvement in EFTS," *Payment Systems Newsletter*, Vol. 6, No. 4, April, 1974, p. 3.

32. Arthur D. Little, Inc., p. 8. The concern of Congress with all aspects of the credit problem was made evident by the January 1975 introduction of H.R. 212 which, among other things, provides for the allocation of credit.
33. See "FHLBB Asks Consumer Lending, Checks at S&Ls," *American Banker,* February 7, 1975, p. 1.
34. Arthur D. Little, Inc., p. 8.
35. Ibid.
36. Ibid.
37. See the landmark study on privacy in a computerized society, *Records, Computers, and the Rights of Citizens,* Report of the Secretary's Advisory Committee on Automated Personal Data Systems, Washington, D.C., July, 1973. Also see Norris, Robert B., "Consumer Record Keeping," *Consumer Credit 1975,* Practising Law Institute, New York, 1975, pp. 59-88; "Cautionary Notes on EFTS," *American Banker,* September 18, 1974, p. 4; "BAI Asks Task Force To Study Banks' Personal Data Use, Draft Ethics Code," *American Banker,* January 30, 1975, pp. 1, 14.
38. Norris, pp. 59-88.
39. *Records, Computers and the Rights of Citizens,* pp. viii-ix.
40. Ibid., pp. xx-xxi.
41. For example, the recently enacted Privacy Act of 1974 (Public Law 93-579) in broad terms provides as follows: (1) Permits an individual access to personal information contained in Federal agency files and to correct or amend the information. (2) Prevents an agency maintaining a file on an individual from using it or making it available to another agency for a second purpose without the individual's consent. (3) Requires Federal agencies to maintain only such records as are relevant and necessary to accomplish their lawfully intended purpose. (4) Requires Federal agencies to collect information where practicable directly from the individual when the information may result in adverse action to the individual. (5) Requires Federal agencies to inform each individual from whom it obtains information on an appropriate form the authority which authorizes the solicitation and whether disclosure is mandatory or voluntary, the purpose for which the information is sought and its intended use, and the consequences to the individual, if any, of not providing the requested information. (6) Requires Federal agencies to publish in the Federal Register annually a notice of the existence and character of all data banks and identifiable information contained therein. (7) Prohibits agencies from keeping records that describe an individual's exercise of First Amendment rights unless the records were authorized by statute or approved by the individual or were within the scope of an official law enforcement activity. (8) Permits an individual to seek injunctive relief to inspect, correct or amend a record maintained by an agency and permits the individual to recover actual damages in a sum not less than

$1,000 and reasonable attorney's fee when an agency acts in a manner which is "intentional or willful." (9) Provides that an officer or employee of an agency who discloses identifiable information to any person or agency not entitled to receive it, or willfully maintains a system of records without meeting the notice requirements of the Act, shall be subject to a fine of not more than $5,000. (10) Provides that any person who knowingly and willfully requests or obtains identifiable information from any agency under false pretenses shall be subject to a fine of not more than $5,000. (11) Exempts from disclosure provisions: records maintained by the Central Intelligence Agency; records maintained by law enforcement agencies; Secret Service records; statistical information; names of persons providing material used for determining the qualification of an individual for federal government service; federal testing or examination material and National Archives historical records. (12) Prohibits an agency from selling or renting an individual's name or address for mailing list use. (13) Requires agencies to provide adequate advance notice to Congress and to the Office of Management and Budget of any proposal to establish or alter any system of records. (14) Requires the President to submit to Congress by June 30 of each year a consolidated report on the number of records exempted by each federal agency and the reasons for the exemptions. (15) Establishes a Privacy Protection Study Commission composed of seven members to provide Congress and the President information about problems related to privacy in the public sector. (16) Makes it illegal for any Federal, state or local agency to deny an individual any benefit provided by law because he refuses to disclose his Social Security account number to the agency, unless required by Federal statute or was required prior to January 1, 1975. (17) Authorizes $1.5 million over the three fiscal years 1975-77 to carry out the functions, studies and duties of the Privacy Protection Study Commission.

Although this Act does not apply to the private sector, the Privacy Protection Study Commission's mandate specifically covers the private sector.

42. The membership of the Commission is as follows: the Chairman of the Board of Governors of the Federal Reserve System or his delegate; the Attorney General or his delegate; the Comptroller of the Currency or his delegate; the Chairman of the Federal Home Loan Bank Board or his delegate; the Administrator of the National Credit Union Administration or his delegate; the Chairman of the Board of Directors of the Federal Deposit Insurance Corporation or his delegate; the Chairman of the Federal Communications Commission or his delegate; the Postmaster General or his delegate; the Secretary of the Treasury or his delegate; the Chairman of the Federal Trade Commission or his delegate; two individuals, appointed by the President, one of whom is an official of a State agency which regulates banking, or

similar financial institutions, and one of whom is an official of a State agency which regulates thrift or similar financial institutions; seven individuals, appointed by the President, who are officers or employees of, or who otherwise represent banking, thrift, or other business entities, including one representative each of commercial banks, mutual savings banks, savings and loan associations, credit unions, retailers, nonbanking institutions offering credit card services, and organizations providing interchange services for credit cards issued by banks; five individuals, appointed by the President, from private life who are not affiliated with, do not represent and have no substantial interest in any banking, thrift, or other financial institution, including but not limited to credit unions, retailers, and insurance companies; the Comptroller General of the United States or his delegate; and the Director of the Office of Technology Assessment.

Chapter 5

1. The reader is referred back to the discussion on payments system costs in Chapter 2. Also see Arthur D. Little, Inc., *An Assessment of Less Cash/Less Check Technology,* National Science Foundation, 1974, Chapters 2, 6; Flannery, Mark J. and Dwight M. Jaffee, *The Economic Implications of an Electronic Monetary Transfer System,* D. C. Heath and Company, Lexington, Massachusetts, 1973, Chapters 4-8.
2. Flannery and Jaffee, p. 81.
3. Ibid., p. 78.
4. The most frequently cited example of this type of relationship is the inordinate dependence of the housing industry on the savings and loan industry.
5. *The Report of the President's Commission on Financial Structure & Regulation,* Washington, D.C., December, 1971, p. 1.
6. Ibid., p. 8. Also see Jones, Oliver H., "Poor Timing, Arguments for Bank, S&L Reforms Peril Grand Objectives," *The Mortgage Banker,* October, 1973, p. 12.
7. Jacobs, Donald P., "Technology in Banking's Future," *The Bankers Magazine,* Vol. 156, No. 3, Summer, 1973, p. 25.
8. "Smith Issues Ruling Granting Electronic Terminals Without Geographic Limitation," *American Banker,* December 13, 1974, pp. 1, 8; 39 Fed. Reg. 44416 (December 24, 1974).
9. *Washington Financial Reports,* December 16, 1974, p. A-6, T-23-21.
10. Jones, pp. 12-13.
11. Ibid. Also, with the recommendations of the Commission serving as a guide, Congress was called upon in 1973 to consider the implementation of the following reforms: The removal of interest rate ceilings on time and savings deposits over a period of 5½ years; The authorization for expanded deposit services for

consumers by federally chartered thrift institutions and banks; The expansion of investment and lending alternatives for federally chartered thrift institutions and banks; The authorization of the federal chartering of stock savings and loan institutions and mutual savings banks; The creation or provision of a central source of funds for credit units; The removal of FHA and VA interest rate ceilings; The modification of the tax structure of banks and thrift institutions.

12. Adamy, Clarence G., "Retail Industry Views on EFTS," speech given at the First Annual Payments System Policy Conference, Chicago, Illinois, December 2, 1974.

13. Ibid.

14. Flannery and Jaffee, pp. 78-79.

(continued from front flap)

In the course of monitoring EFTS developments for the National Consumer Finance Association and as a regular participant in the Treasury Department's planning conferences on direct deposit-electronic funds transfer program for recurring federal payments, Dr. Bender is familiar with many of the developments which are rapidly progressing from plans to the realities of daily life.

EFTS gives force to the author's contention that these developments "portend revolutionary changes in traditional economic and social relationships—changes which will far transcend those historically associated with the evolution of the exchange mechanism."

* * *

Mark G. Bender is Economist at the National Consumer Finance Association, Washington, D.C., and is editor of NCFA's monthly economic newsletter *Finance Facts* and the author of the NCFA quarterly *Installment Credit Indicators.* He received his Ph.D. degree from the University of Connecticut.